China's New Education Experiment in Action

WORKS BY
ZHU YONGXIN
ON
EDUCATION

China's New Education
Experiment in Action

ZHU YONGXIN

New York   Chicago   San Francisco   Athens   London
Madrid   Mexico City   Milan   New Delhi
Singapore   Sydney   Toronto

1 2 3 4 5 6 7 8 9   LSI   23 22 21 20 19 18

Beijing Jinghua Hucais Printing, Co., Ltd.

ISBN   978-1-260-45249-5
MHID   1-260-45249-2

e-ISBN   978-1-260-45250-1
e-MHID   1-260-45250-6

B&R Book Program

McGraw-Hill Education books are available at special quantity discounts to use as premiums and sales promotions or for use in corporate training programs. To contact a representative, please visit the Contact Us pages at www.mhprofessional.com.

Contents

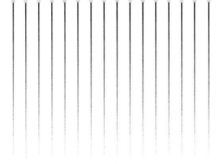

1

The Origin, Evolution, and Vision of the New Education Experiment

I. The Origin of the New Education Experiment
II. The Evolution of the New Education Experiment
III. The Vision of the New Education Experiment

Reform of China's education sector has been in full swing since the 1980s. The new curriculum reform in the public sector and the new basic education experiment in the private sector are reshaping our education to a varying degree. In particular, since the twenty-first century, the education reform has been taking more and more forms, including the classroom reform represented by Dulangkou Middle School, the curriculum reform represented by Beijing No. 11 Middle School, the explorations of private schools such as Montessori and Waldorf, and the emergence of home schooling and the idea of "self-help through education."

Among all these exploratory practices, the New Education Experiment has taken on a unique path and stood out among others.

I. The Origin of the New Education Experiment
The conception of the New Education Experiment can be traced back to the late 1980s.

From 1986, I spent nearly five years writing the book *Studies on Chinese Thoughts on Education: The Achievements and Contributions of Chinese*

Education Science. During that period, I read extensively, including books written by representative figures of the New Education Movement in the West and books on education written by ancient and contemporary Chinese educators. The encounter with these lofty ideals on education inspired me to create and deliver an ideal education of my times. The book left me with a new mission.

In 1988, I was commissioned by Guangxi People's Publishing House to write the book *The Dilemma and the Way Out: Comments on Education in Contemporary China*. To write this book, I collected an ocean of information and materials about education in China. While excited about the achievements made since the implementation of the reform and opening up policy, I was anxious about the growing shortage of funding and the deterioration of exam-oriented education. Upset by the huge contrast between the ideal and the reality, I was eager to make a difference for China's education.

In 1990, I spent a year at the Sophia University in Japan as a visiting scholar. I worked at an institute that specialized in the studies of German-speaking cultures, but I spent nearly all the time observing Japan's education. After returning to China, I chaired the compilation of the *Book Series on Education in Contemporary Japan*. Comprised of 12 volumes, it systematically introduces Japan's preschool education, primary education, higher education, and vocational education and studies Japans' education reform and development since the Meiji Reform, especially since the end of the Second World War. A close look at our neighbor country lent me some deep thoughts on our own education reform.

In 1993, I was appointed the head of academic affairs of Suzhou University, the youngest appointed in a comprehensive university in China. While in office, I introduced the must-read book program, the incentive major/minor program, the credit system, the pilot program for the reform of liberal arts education, and the experimental program for strengthening natural science education, accumulating experience to build a campus full of the fragrance of books.

At the end of 1997, I was transferred to work as the deputy mayor in charge of education and culture for the Municipal People's Government of Suzhou. Pressured by the public criticism of exam-oriented education and the huge gap between education reform and the economic reform, and inspired by regional education reform, I started to picture what the ideal education should be like. Accordingly I launched action plans to reform disadvantaged schools, to learn from model teachers and headmasters, to modernize rural primary schools, and to promote information technology in the education sector, and made Suzhou one of the first Chinese cities to popularize nine-year compulsory education. These actions considerably improved the quality of local education and the morale of teachers, and stimulated me to continue with education reform.

In 1999, I started to read books about management, including *The World According to Peter Drucker*. It turned out to be life-changing for me. I was struck by a story from the book. One day, Drucker, accompanied by his father, went to visit his teacher, Mr. Schumpeter, another master of management. Schumpeter said to the Druckers that, "In my age, I know that to have my name remembered by future generations, my books and theories alone are insufficient. They are of no significance unless they can change people's life." It suddenly dawned on me that despite all the books I had written, I didn't actually get involved in the life of education, not to mention affect or change teachers' lives. So I decided to change the way I talk, the way I do things, to truly get involved with the teachers and the life of education.

But it's easier said than done, to get down from the ivory tower and dive into real life. I needed an intermediary. I needed to change not only how I think and how I feel, but also how I work. That summer, as I contemplated a change, Jiangsu Education News Press convened a conference on innovative education in Suzhou and asked me to share my view on what an ideal teacher should be with the delegates. Through that speech, I found the way to express my thoughts on education and the way to relate to teachers and the life of education. After the speech, I was invited to share my education ideal with young teachers at Hutangqiao Central Primary School in Wujin, Jiangsu.

In 2000, I published *My Ideal on Education* based on my lectures given in Suzhou and Hutangqiao Central Primary School, systematically putting forth some goals of ideal education. The book kindled the passion for education among numerous teachers. Some dismissed it as an ideal that would never come true because the hands of principals and teachers are tied in the exam-oriented education system, but I believed that the wisdom of education lie in spotting the potential for greatest development in a limited space. In the same institutional environment, some schools and teachers were doing exceptionally well while most others were dawdling away. The biggest difference is their initiative. By then, I had naturally come up with this idea of founding a school and exploring a new path of education for the country.

In September 2002, Yufeng Experimental School of Kunshan, the first school of the New Education Experiment, was founded in Suzhou, and the experiment was underway.

II. The Evolution of the New Education Experiment

My Ideal on Education was published in November 2000, an event that marked the birth of the New Education Experiment, not only because the book directly conceived the experiment, but also because the book provided thoughts and ideas for getting started.

At first, we considered calling the experiment the Ideal Education Experiment, but gave it up for fear it might be confusing and misunderstood as an education experiment about ideals. After rounds of discussions and careful deliberation, we decided on the name the New Education Experiment, paying tribute to academic predecessors and previous theories. In 1889, British educator Cecil Reddie founded Abbotsholme School and started the New School (Education) Movement in Europe. The movement then swept across the world, started progressive thought in the United States, and exerted great influence on China's education reform in the 1920s and 1930s. It bore great influence on many great schools including the Summerhill School founded by A. S. Neil, the Bus Study Garden founded by Japanese new-style educator Sousaku Kobayashi, the University of Chicago Laboratory Schools founded by John Dewey, and many big names in modern education history, such as Russell, Percy Nunn, Montessori, Piaget, Whitehead, Dewey, Tao Xingzhi, and Chen Heqin.

The New Education Experiment in China in the early twenty-first century can be seen as an echo of the New Education Movement in contemporary China in the era of globalization. The two have some features in common: they both aim to reflect on, criticize, and reconstruct education in reality and advocate respect for children's individuality and freedom. They have led to the opening of a number of experimental schools and tried to reform and innovate in both education and society. In addition, both are initiated by the private sector. In this sense, the New Education Experiment is a link and extension of the New Education Movement, with the label "experiment" to differentiate it from the latter.

The development history of the New Education Experiment can be divided into three stages. The preliminary stage, from September 1999 to September 2002, was driven mainly by ideals, passion, and thoughts. My lectures given at Hutangqiao Central Primary School and the proposal of basic ideas about my education ideal inspired the idea of the New Education Experiment. The publication of *My Ideal of Education* marked the conception of the experiment. In June 2002, we set up a website dedicated to the New Education Experiment, the ideas of which aroused the passion of many principals and teachers for education.

The deepening stage, from September 2002 to July 2013, was driven by the curriculum and programs, and extended by training and on-site activities. In September 2002, Yufeng Experimental School of Kunshan, the first school of the New Education Experiment, was opened, and *The New Education Dream* was published, marking the full launch of the experiment.

At Yufeng Experimental School, we proposed five viewpoints: (1) Let teachers and students have dialogues with the noble human spirit; (2) teach things that will be helpful for the rest of students' lives; (3) demonstrate complete belief in the potential of students and teachers; (4) value the mental state and advocate success experience; and (5) stress individuality development and focus on character education. We also proposed five actions: (1) Create a campus with the fragrance of books; (2) encourage teachers and students to write essays together; (3) listen to the voice outside the window; (4) provide bilingual eloquence training; (5) build a digital community. Thanks to online dissemination of the viewpoints, some other schools joined Yufeng Experimental School in the experiment. Meanwhile, we formed five task forces in Suzhou to implement the five actions and promote the research of the experiment.

In July 2003, the New Education Experiment held its first seminar in Yufeng Experimental School, naming its first group of experimental schools. In April 2004, the kickoff meeting for the Studies of Practice and Promotion of the New Education Theory, a major research program under the National Tenth Five-Year Plan for the Education Science took place in Zhangjiagang High School and Hutangqiao Central Primary School in Jiangsu Province. The kickoff meeting was considered the second seminar of the New Education Experiment. In July, the third seminar was convened at the building of Xiangyu Education Group in Baoying County, Jiangsu. In May and September that year, Jiangyan Municipal Bureau of Education in Jiangsu and Qiaoxi District Government of Shijiazhuang, Hebei Province, designated their own county-level experimental zones for new education, driving the local experiment with administrative forces.

In November 2003, the New Education Experiment Research Center was inaugurated in Yufeng Experimental School. In June 2005, the Research Center co-compiled the *Walk with the Ideal: The Guiding Book for the New Education Experiment* with the research group, adding "Construct the ideal classroom" to the five actions. This was followed by the publication of *Book Series on New Education*. In July, the fourth seminar was held at Yandao Street Foreign Language School in Chengdu, Sichuan Province, with the theme "New Moral Education." At the meeting, the New Citizenship Reader was released, introducing new citizens and new life education into the New Education Experiment. In December, the Spring of North-National Seminar on the New Education Experiment and Specialized Growth of Teachers was convened at Jilin No.1 Elementary Primary School, proposing the three-professional model of the New Education Experiment. This seminar was also considered the fifth seminar of the New Education Experiment.

In 2006, a number of outstanding young teachers from primary and middle schools joined the New Education Research Center, responsible for research and promotion of the experiment. They injected vitality into the experiment and were committed to curriculum development, training, and promotion of New Education. In July, the sixth seminar was held at the auditorium of Tsinghua University, undertaken by Beijing 61 Middle School, Primary School Affiliated to Tsinghua University and Zhongguancun No. 1 Primary School. At the meeting, the core value of New Education was proposed: "live a happy, complete life of education."

In just a few years, the New Education Experiment expanded to involve more than one million students and more than 60,000 teachers in over 500 experimental schools in 14 experimental zones, distributed in over 20 provinces and municipalities including Jiangsu, Zhejiang, Beijing, Hubei, Hunan, Shaanxi, Jilin, Guangdong, Shanxi, Anhui, Hebei, and Henan.

In November 2006, the first working meeting of experimental zones was held in Xiuzhou District, Jiaxing City of Zhejiang Province, to summarize the experience and tactics in promoting the New Education Experiment at the regional level.

In July 2007, the seventh seminar was held in Yuncheng, Shanxi Province, with the theme "Reading, Writing and Living Together," and launched programs including the "Reading in the Morning and at Noon and Reflecting in the Evening: The New Education Lifestyle for Children," and the "Caterpillar and Butterfly: The New Education Child Reading Program." A number of outstanding teachers shared touching stories of new education. As the experiment continued to expand in size, in addition to academic studies and professional promotion, there were many matters to manage and coordinate. Thus to better serve participants of the experiment, we founded the New Education Institute as a key management body for the New Education Experiment.

In November 2007, the New Education Research Association, or the Specialized Committee on Studies of the New Education Experiment of Jiangsu Education Association, was founded in Haimen. At the founding ceremony, I proposed the Spirit of New Education as idealism, awareness of fieldwork, teamwork, and public interest.

In July 2008, the eighth seminar was held in Cangnan, Wenzhou of Zhejiang Province. It summarized experience in constructing the ideal classroom, and proposed three standards for the ideal classroom and the viewpoint of "deep resonance between knowledge, life, and living." In December, the research program on the tactics for the New Education Experiment and Education for All-round Development was designated a major research program under the national Eleventh Five-Year Plan for Education Science. From then on, the New Education Experiment started to explore the path toward education for all-around development.

In July 2009, with the theme "Write Down the Teachers' Life Legend," the ninth seminar was held in Haimen, Jiangsu Province. Based on the life narration theory and the three-professional theory, it compared professional identity and specialized development as the two wings for the growth of teachers.

The tenth seminar took place in Qiaoxi District, Shijiazhuang, Hebei Province in July 2010 with the theme "Culture: The Soul of a School." In September, the New Reading Institute was inaugurated in Beijing. It then released basic reading lists for primary school students, for preschool children, for junior middle school students, for high school students, and for entrepreneurs, and rose to be an influential reading list developer. In the second year after its inauguration, the New Reading Institute was awarded the honor of National Reading Promoter. In December, the Jiangsu Changming Education Foundation, or the New Education Foundation, a fund-raising body for the New Education Experiment, was founded.

In July 2011, the First International Summit on New Education was convened at Hutangqiao Central Primary School in Wujin, Jiangsu Province, including experts and educators from the United States and Japan to exchange views on field survey of education and marking the start of international exchange for the New Education Experiment. In September, the eleventh seminar, themed on "Bring out the Essence of Chinese Culture," took place in Dongsheng District, Ordos, Inner Mongolia. In November, the New Education Parent-Child Reading Research Center was founded in Beijing, then renamed New Parents Institute, to study and promote the work related to family–school cooperation and family education. The Firefly Work Station was then opened in more than 40 Chinese cities, organizing more than 5,000 public-interest activities for tens of thousands of teachers and parents, and tracking and serving the growth of more than 900 seed teachers across the country for years.

The twelfth seminar, themed "Create the Ideal Classroom," took place in Linzi, Shandong Province in July 2012. In October, the Second International Summit on New Education, under the theme "Education and Cultural Reconstruction," was held at Xiaoshi Middle School, Ningbo, Zhejiang Province. The summit increased the basic actions of the New Education Experiment to ten, with the addition of one thing per month, create the ideal classroom, develop an excellent curriculum, and family–school cooperation.

In March 2013, the New Education Academy for Teachers' Growth, or the Haimen New Education Training Center, was founded with the approval of the city government of Nantong, and it rapidly grew into China's major new education base for idea training and program promotion. In less than three years, it trained nearly 40,000 participants in more than 100 batches. By July 2013, the New Education Experiment had involved more than 125,400 teachers and more than 1.86 million students from 1,764 experimental schools in 40 experimental zones in 23 Chinese provinces/municipalities/autonomous regions.

The third stage, improvement, has run from July 2013 to today. It has been marked by systematic development of the new education curriculum and the enrichment and improvement of the theoretical framework.

In July 2013, the thirteenth seminar, themed "Develop Excellent Curriculum," took place in Xiaoshan, Zhejiang Province, proposing the curriculum framework for the New Education Experiment, which was to develop new citizenship education, new artistic education, new intellectual education, and characteristic courses on top of the new life education. By then, the theoretical framework and the action and program system of the New Education Experiment had begun to take shape, and the experiment's influence had expanded. In November 2013, the third International Summit on New Education was held in Chengdu, bringing together noted educators from around the world to discuss the topic "The Power of Reading."

In April 2014, the working meeting of experimental zones was held in Qingyang City, Gansu Province, witnessing the changes brought by the New Education Experiment to the education scene in West China. In July, the fourteenth seminar, with the theme "Artistic Education for the Pursuit of Beauty," took place in Suzhou, bringing the New Education Experiment back to its origin 14 years after its initiation. In November, the fourth International Summit on New Education, themed "Construct the Ideal Classroom," took place in Rizhao, Shandong Province, inviting educators, scholars, and teachers from at home and abroad to discuss the paths and tactics for building the ideal classroom.

In January 2015, the narration seminar for creating the ideal classroom was held at Beijing Normal University. It was attended by noted professors including Tao Xiping, Shi Zhongying, and Liu Tiefang and director Wang Dinghua of the Basic Education Department of the Ministry of Education, who spoke highly of the classroom created by model teachers of new education. In May, the working meeting of experimental zones was held in Kuitun, Xinjiang, witnessing the flourishing of new education in border areas. The experiment conducted in regions inhabited by ethnic minorities had become a highlight of regional education. In July, the fifteenth seminar, themed "Increase the Length, Width, and Height of Life," was held in Jintang County, Chengdu, Sichuan Province, gathering more than 2,000 delegates from across the country to discuss the unique role of new life education in post-disaster reconstruction. In November, the International Forum on New Education, with the theme "Develop Excellent Curriculum," took place in Guancheng District, Zhengzhou, Henan Province, showcasing the theoretical explorations and practices in new education curriculum development.

In April 2016, the working meeting of experimental zones took place in Suixian County, Hubei Province. Suixian joined the New Education Experiment in 2011, and in just five years, it realized leapfrog development in local education and created a miracle in rural education. There were 73 junior middle schools in Suizhou City. Of the 25 in Suixian County, 23 were rated among the top 30 in the city: 14 in the top 20 and 7 in the top 10. In July, the sixteenth seminar, themed "Foster Second Nature through Habit Cultivation," took place in Zhucheng, gathering nearly 2,000 delegates from the education sector to discuss the One Thing per Month program. Zhucheng City joined the New Education Experiment as a whole in 2012 and considered new education a priority for promoting local education reform and development. The number of experimental schools has increased from 26 in 2012 to 409, and all subject teachers, families, and other community members are encouraged to engage in the New Education Experiment. In November, the International Summit on New Education was held in Xiangyu Middle School in Wenzhou, Zhejiang Province, where we shared our thoughts on future education with scholars from the United States, Singapore, and Finland.

In the past 17 years, the New Education Experiment has scored remarkable achievements in studies and promotion. So far, it has engaged more than 3.7 million teachers and students from nearly 3,500 experimental schools in more than 100 county-level experimental zones across the country.

The New Education Experiment has also gained extensive attention from the international academia. In 2008, the book *The Boiling Education Reform in China* published by the Research Institute for Oriental Cultures of Gakushuin University gave a systematic account of China's New Education Experiment. In 2009, I was invited by the Brain Korea project team in the Republic of Korea to give a lecture about "Living a Happy, Complete Life of Education" at Chonbuk National University. Later, the ten-volume *A Collection of Zhu Yongxin's Lectures on Education* was translated and published in Korean. In 2014, the New Education Experiment was voted among the 15 finalists for the World Innovation for Education Award by the Qatar Foundation. In 2016, McGraw-Hill Education Group purchased the global copyright of 16 books on new education, including *New Education in China*, and had published all of them by the end of 2015.

In 2016, a research team headed by Dr. Ye Renmin from the Houston Department of Education in the United States found through big data analysis that students receiving new education outperform students in ordinary schools in terms of the sense of belonging in school and comprehensive reading capabilities, and the gap is obvious. The research report pointed out that "[f]or such a massive education experiment that involves so many students across the country, the New Education Experiment delivers a better campus feeling and experience for students, and improves their interest and competency in reading and their reading habit. Thus the efficacy and beauty of the experiment is praiseworthy." In April 2016, I was invited to give a keynote speech on China's New Education Experiment at the China Education Forum held at Harvard University and the Sino-U.S. Education Forum held at the Massachusetts Institute of Technology.

III. The Vision of the New Education Experiment

The New Education Experiment is marked by idealism and field actions. While upholding the banner of idealism and awakening teachers' passion for life and education, it places special emphasis on field awareness and the spirit of doers. Actions such as "Create a Campus with the Fragrance of Books," "Teachers and Students Write Essays Together," "Listen to the Voice outside the Window," "Bilingual Eloquence Training," "Build a Digital Community," "Develop Excellent Curriculum," "Create the Ideal Classroom," "One Thing per Month," and "Family–School Cooperation," advocate the lifestyle of "reading in the morning and at noon and reflecting in the evening." These initiatives have given rise to original courses on listening, reading, painting, narration, and life narratives and has provided direction for teachers' growth through professional identity, professional reading, professional writing, and professional community. It endeavors to change students' living status, the way teachers work, the way schools develop, and the way research on education is conducted, and it has made some progress.

In the early stage of the experiment, our goals were summarized as:

1. To become a paradise of growth for students
2. To create an ideal stage for the growth of teachers
3. To provide an ideal platform for schools to improve education quality
4. To become the spiritual home and the ideal village for the new education community

This is a poetic statement of the four goals of the experiment. Later, the four goals were condensed into two visions: to raise a flag of education for all-around development in China, and to foster the New Education School that is deeply rooted in the Chinese society.

These two visions are shared by all practitioners of new education.

Vision 1: To raise a flag of education for all-around development in China. Despite all the big talk over the years about education for all-around development, in reality, exam-oriented education still prevails. The root cause is that we have many theories about education for all-around development but too few actions. Despite all the controversy and disagreement on what education for all-around development is, which is further complicated by the idea of "core qualities," we believe there are three universal standards. First, education for all-around development should be for all students, coinciding with our idea that new education is for all people. Second, education for all-around development should promote students' development in all aspects, closely linked to our idea that education benefits every human aspect as well as our development theory and lofty ideal theory. Third, education for all-around development should be sustainable, echoing our idea that we should teach students things that are helpful in their lifetime. Therefore, the New Education Experiment is an attempt and exploration of education for all-around development.

More importantly, the New Education Experiment is taking concrete actions to lay the foundation for education for all-around development. The most important quality of a person is his capacity for spiritual growth, and one's history of spiritual growth can be tracked from his reading history. Hence education for all-around development should start from reading, and reading should be the cornerstone of education for all-around development. We must promote reading so as to translate our huge population into human resources assets. Without reading, there's no education for all-around development. Why did we take so many detours in promoting education for all-around development? Because we mistook it as specialty education, such as artistic education like playing musical instruments and singing. We should avoid the same mistake in the promotion of core qualities. Since the content of the New Education Experiment is what education for all-around development needs, the experiment should naturally become a prominent flag of education for this development.

Vision 2: To foster a New Education School that is deeply rooted in the Chinese society by constructing the theoretical system, the curriculum system, and campus culture of New Education. China's contribution to the world's education is far from enough. Throughout global education history, only a few Chinese educators have left their marks, such as Confucius and Tao Xingzhi. Nearly everything we talk about is quoted or borrowed from the West, such as constructivism, cognitive theories, humanism, and multiple intelligences, and we are walking under the shadows of Duway, Bruner, Babansky, and Suhomlinski. Little of what we say is homegrown. It would be such a regret if we the Chinese fail to make our due contribution to the world's education scene. We practitioners of New Education take it as our responsibility to explore our own theory, find our own style, build up our own brand, and contribute to the world's education through our concrete actions at home.

There is a long way to go, but we firmly believe that the visions are attainable. We have favorable conditions for the fostering of the New Education School. First, though we don't have the University of Chicago Laboratory Schools founded by Duway or the Pavlysh School founded by Suhomlinski, we have more than 3,500 experimental schools across China. We are working on standards for these experimental schools and are planning to develop some model schools. Second, of all the experts in the New Education Institute and teachers of experimental schools, we believe some will stand out and leave marks in Chinese education history. Third, with all the experimental schools and specialists in New Education, I believe we will be able to see some masterpieces on New Education soon. Stop complaining about the exam-oriented system. Let's enjoy the dance in fetters. Every individual counts, every class counts, and every student counts. The future of China's education lies in the hands of every one of us, in every class we have, and in every minute we have with students. Let's make the most of them.

Guided by these two visions, in the near future, we will be able to see such students graduating from new education experimental schools: they cherish a political ideal, earn their money through hard work, put people first in scientific studies, and indulge themselves within moral restraints. This is what we are working for. We need to continue working hard and be always on the way to attain these grand visions.

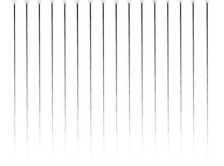

2

The Ideas, Spirit, and Actions of the New Education Experiment

What is new education? In the eyes of many practitioners, it is first a dream of reform, a kind of passion for growth. Yes, the New Education Experiment does demand from its participants religious piety, passion, expectation for and trust in education and life. It snowballs by awakening more and more people. Passion arouses more passion, and dream inspires more dreams. The New Education Experiment looks for persons sharing the same ideal across the country, offers them effective courses, allows them to translate dreams and passion into noticeable educational achievements, and thus turns them into role models. Then these role models are encouraged to share their stories with and inspire others. Therefore, it's fair to say that the New Education Experiment is distinctly marked by its stress on educational utopia, idealism, passion, dream, and vocational identity, without all of which, the experiment would cease to exist.

Some media used to understand new education as spiritual education. They believed that compared with exam-oriented education, which places scores above everything else, new education calls attention to the dialogue with the noble human spirit, emphasizes that one's spiritual development history is reflected in one's reading history, and advocates to cultivate a benevolent and sensitive heart and reshape the spiritual world of students by "reading in the morning and at noon and reflecting in the evening."

But what is the academic definition of new education?

I. The Core Idea of the New Education Experiment: Live a Happy, All-Around Educational Life

We define the New Education Experiment as an educational experiment that proceeds from teachers' growth, features ten major actions including creating a campus full of the fragrance of books, and aims to help teachers and students live a happy and all-around educational life. Its core value lies with the happy and all-around educational life.

We hold that education should of course be future-oriented, but also relevant to now. Education reflects the way we live, the way we behave. As a path toward a good life, education should be enjoyable and enable all participants to live a contented, complete life.

The New Education Experiment's stress on the importance of living a happy, all-around educational life demonstrates its reflection on the ultimate meaning of education, and of course its concerns and discontent about current educational issues. To our regret, in many places, education has taken the carefree childhood away from students and left them only with frustrations. Many children have lost their curiosity about the world, the passion and desire to follow their ideal, the courage for trying, and the gratitude for what they have. What do we need education for if it delivers no joy to our students and teachers?

We hold that the educational life should be not just happy, but also complete. The reason is that one-sided emphasis on happiness would misdirect all the attention to feelings or cause the false impression that emotional pleasure is the most important. In today's world, education is mostly distorted, one-sided, and values scores above everything else. But the biggest problem is that it underestimates moral education. In fact, the aim of education is to cultivate good human nature and then create a beautiful society. The human life should be complete in the biological, social, and spiritual dimensions. Education is complete only when it can stretch the life's length, width, and depth. A man is complete only when he becomes himself. To cultivate a complete human being is the highest pursuit of education, and of course what we new education practitioners are ultimately after. That's why we advocate that the school should be the hub of great things where students can encounter good things, spot good things, and become good human beings.

II. The Philosophical, Psychological, and Ethical Basis for the New Education Experiment

Corresponding to the ontology, values, and methodologies of education, the New Education Experiment has its own philosophical, ethical, and psychological basis. Its philosophical basis is built on development and actions; its psychological basis on status, potential, and individuality, which is also the basic approach it takes; and its ethical basis on nobleness and harmony, which are the ideal of the experiment.

i. The Philosophical Basis

The philosophical basis of the New Education Experiment is built on development and actions. "For all people and for everything of people" used to be the experiment's statement of core value. We care about not just students, but also teachers, principals, parents, and all other people engaged in education. We care about not just scores, but also the character, the soul, and growth.

We advocate to proceed from every individual life, set educational goals, and carry out educational activities to meet the needs of individual development. We hope to, through human-oriented knowledge and education, guide every individual engaged in education to develop his personality, be himself, be a true human being, and eventually accomplish self-realization.

"For all people" echoes the call of "education for all," and "for everything of people" implies that education is for the completeness of human beings, to cultivate humans of all-around, harmonious development, not "well-trained dogs."

The New Education Experiment is all about actions. We believe in "no pain, no gain" and "only persistence can work wonders." Many educational theories are too far from practice and real life. The New Education Experiment values actions more than theories and endeavors to change educational behavior. This is what differentiates it from many other educational experiments. We are not saying that other experiments are only about talk, not actions, but that their actions are not as popular, doable, and welcomed by participants as those of the New Education Experiment.

For example, to change teachers' educational behavior, the New Education Experiment encourages them to keep an educational diary and write educational stories, cases, and essays. Such self-reflection serves as a wake-up call for teachers and will motivate them to pursue career development. The New Education Experiment sweeps across primary and middle schools with its unique charm that separates it from previous educational experiments. Its humanistic spirit and its practical, feasible actions free of vanity and falsehood drastically change educational practice. Inspired by the new education ideal, the dormant desire for change and progress is aroused among teachers who throw themselves into new education actions and enjoy themselves while doing so.

Persistence is the key to successful actions. The implementation of the experiment will keep winnowing out those who give up halfway. That's why we stress the importance of persistence so much. Only those who are persistent can work wonders and make a real difference.

ii. The Psychological Basis

The psychological basis of the New Education Experiment is on status, potential, and individuality. The mental state and the experience of success are vital for new education actions. People in a good mental state can motivate themselves and thus keep working hard. The New Education Experiment tries to deliver a positive educational experience for students and based on that, encourage them to aim higher. School education should enable students to experience success over and over, so as to increase their self-confidence and willingness to challenge themselves. The success of a student must no longer be measured by exam scores alone. We should advocate new values of success and motivate students with the experience of success.

An important mission of the New Education Experiment is to awaken teachers and students to their own potential and motivate them to achieve greater success. We believe their potential can never be overestimated. Only with confidence can teachers and students fully tap their potential, showcase their talents, and have a peak experience. A very important job of teachers is to boost the confidence of students and encourage them to pursue excellence and become successful. Self-confidence is also the source of educational creativity and wisdom of teachers.

Hence the New Education Experiment advocates absolute trust in the potential of teachers and students and the need to create space for their growth. We believe that the bigger the stage, the more brilliant their performance; the more space they have, the more achievements they will deliver.

The New Education Experiment celebrates individuality and unique characteristics. We hope each school will develop its own characteristics, as will each student and teacher. Let everyone be himself. We always believe that being special is being excellent, and the best is always the most special.

Individual development includes the discovery of one's potential character, aura, interests, feelings and thinking, respect for one's spiritual liberty and uniqueness, and encouragement for one's critical, unique, and original thinking. In short, it means respect and development of psychological differences among individuals.

Specialty is what makes you exceptional. It is developed based on the full respect for and development of individual personality, under the care of schools and the whole society, and reinforced in the process of one's growth. You do well at school, I am a good dancer, and he has beautiful handwriting. When everyone has his own specialty, he is not inferior to anyone else, and his personality and spiritual world is complete.

iii. The Ethical Basis

The ethical basis of the New Education Experiment is built on nobleness and harmony. Educational purposes are divided into two categories: possible purposes and necessary purposes. The first includes purposes related to the job the student might take after growing up, or "purposes to be established when students enter adulthood." The second refers to the highest and the most fundamental purposes of education, or moral, ethical purposes. J. F. Herbart once pointed out that, "Morality is universally recognized as the highest purpose of human beings, and thus it is also the highest purpose of education." He also noted, "The only work and the whole work of education can be condensed in the concept—morality."

Our education is off track by this standard. We have been lost for a long time. We don't know what education is for or what good education is. We are blind to the ethical purpose of education, a simple but fundamental issue.

The New Education Experiment believes that education is about the cultivation of human beings; through cultivation, it allows teachers and students to have a dialogue with the noble human spirit and then inspires them to pursue lofty ideals and create a better life. The most important job of education is to promote this dialogue, cultivate good human nature and character, and enable students to create a beautiful life. This is where education, and therefore educational reform, should start.

The New Education Experiment advocates that education should be responsible for the rest of the student's life, for his survival and development in the twenty-first century, and for his harmonious development, free spirit, and capacity of independent learning.

The New Education Experiment holds that life has more things that outweigh academic performance, such as one's habits, skills, and lifestyle. We advocate the cultivation of eloquence because we believe it is one of the most important skills for your life. No matter which line of work you are in, you need to communicate and exchange with others, and eloquence really matters. But under the current educational system, schools are too focused on the passing of basic knowledge and the cultivation of basic skills, and in classrooms, teachers do almost all the talking and rarely give students the chance to speak their mind. Then how can students foster and master critical skills such as eloquence?

In the same line of thinking, the New Education Experiment also stresses the importance of reading, writing, reflection, and e-learning, which are all important for one's life. The habit of reading and writing will give you the capacity of lifetime learning; it is a powerful weapon for your self-development.

III. The Spiritual Pursuit of the New Education Experiment

I am often asked, sometimes even by myself, such questions: What drives a non-governmental organization like the New Education Experiment to "wipe the stars" in its pursuit of the happy, all-around educational life it advocates? And what supports you to keep charging ahead on the path to new education?

My answer is that it's the spirit of idealism that is in the DNA of the new education community. To be specific, the new education spirit has four dimensions.

i. Persistent Pursuit of the Ideal

The New Education Experiment is launched to pursue our educational ideal. For its participants, the ideal is bigger than themselves; they strive to elevate themselves by bringing the whole mankind closer to nobility. They know someone has to "wipe the stars" for the world, and they are willing to dedicate their prime youth and wisdom to it.

They are persistent and resilient. No matter what challenges, setbacks, and failures they encounter, they will keep their head up and continue walking. They believe that every individual counts, no matter how insignificant you think you are, and that every individual can make a difference and increase the goodness of the world.

In a book I edited, I included the article entitled "How Big Can I Be?" written by Mr. Zhang Taiyan. Mr. Zhang was a maverick and sometimes called a freak, but he was not angry, but rather happy to hear it. He believed that people with creativity often looked strange to and behaved differently from ordinary people; otherwise they would not be able to endure all their hardships and setbacks in original thinking. For this reason, he admitted that he was a "freak" and would like to infect others with such "freakiness."

I am called a freak too by some people because they think I am too absorbed in promoting new education, and my followers are ridiculed by them as stupid. Like Zhang Taiyan, I take that as a compliment. In my mind, only a persistent, idealist person can qualify for such "freakiness" and "stupidity."

Without persistence, the ideal of new education will not go far. Persistence is like a magic seed and idealism is the fertile soil. When the two meet, they will make an amazing spring.

ii. The Awareness of Fieldwork

In nearly every sector, you can see three kinds of people: bureaucrats, intellectuals, and farmers. With only bureaucrats and intellectuals, the New Education Experiment would never succeed. We need "farmers" who get their hands dirty and engage with students in classrooms day by day.

Almost all the great educators in history were persons of action. I once wrote an essay after reading the biography *Liang Suming's Lonely Thoughts*. In that article, I proclaim that I am not a man of books, but a man of action. Almost all the educators remembered by posterity were persons of action, or more exactly, persons of books and action.

Hence I'm gratified to see how our team members embrace fieldwork. The awareness of fieldwork is in our DNA. We must treasure it and carry it forward. Writing articles and doing research behind closed doors often result in nothing.

I once read an article about how noted professors in India busy themselves with fieldwork and getting their hands dirty instead of just touring around to give lectures. It mentioned Gandhi as an example, who traveled extensively to pursue his ideal.

New education practitioners need to do fieldwork. The articles we write and the activities we organize must all come from the classroom, from first-hand experience. We ask teachers and students to write essays together, not to train them into writers, but to cultivate their passion for life. You need to take actions and make a difference so that you can have things to say in your essay. I hope that every participant of the New Education Experiment could listen to their inner voice in fieldwork and in day-to-day contacts with students, reflect on their daily educational life, and foster the awareness of fieldwork.

iii. Collaboration

We are persistent in the pursuit of our ideal, practical in our actions, and collaborative in interpersonal relations.

All members are equal in the new education community; they all share the same title: teacher. In this community, no one is bossed around or belittled; ideas are exchanged on an equal footing and "arguments" are for genuine, justifiable purposes.

Our team believes only in truth and never bends to any worldly authority. Equality is the prerequisite for truth seeking. In today's world, you cannot go far on your own, no matter how resourceful you are. We must always remember the idea of community and the teamwork spirit. We are bounded by a shared vision, ideal, and pursuit, so even though we live in different parts of the country and might not know each other, we are "living together" in the same family.

On our team, there is an organizational structure, but no administrative pressure; we might argue intensively, but we don't gang up against others; we might disagree, but we respect each other's difference. Only in an equal, truth-seeking, and collaborative atmosphere can the team grow and flourish.

iv. Philanthropy

I have recommended the book *How to Change the World* by David Bornstein to many people. The heroes of the book are some ordinary teachers, lawyers, and doctors in the United States. Some of them invented a home care practice for AIDS patients, some promoted the government to change the medical and healthcare policy, some brought electricity to tens of thousands of rural households in remote areas of developing countries, and some protected numerous acres of prairie. They are ordinary people and they care for other ordinary people like them. Their spirit is called philanthropy.

The New Education Experiment was born out of this philanthropic spirit. It is a treasure whose value we should not only maintain, but also increase.

When I visited Taiwan, I was deeply impressed by the work by the Tzu Chi Foundation. This is a remarkable organization whose mission is to relieve the suffering of those in need and create a better world for all by pooling the love, wisdom, and efforts of people from around the globe. Unlike the New Education Experiment, it is rooted in Buddhist philosophy, but its philanthropic spirit is worth our learning. We need to go to remote rural areas where we are needed the most. Only when we make positive differences there can we say China's education is turning for better.

To sum up, the mission of the New Education Experiment and the essence of the new education spirit are to serve China's education and the Chinese people through the persistent, collaborative pursuit of our ideal and with concrete fieldwork and philanthropic activities.

IV. The Ten Major Actions of the New Education Experiment

The New Education Experiment has labeled itself as a campaign of action since its birth because we know what China needs today are not critics or theorists, but men of action. When launched in the Yufeng Experimental School of Kunshan in 2002, the experiment proposed five major actions, namely, "Create a Campus with the Fragrance of Books," "Teachers and Students Write Essays Together," "Eloquence Training," "Listen to the Voice outside the Window," and "Build a Digital Community." Later we added "Deliver the Ideal Class" and proposed the 6+1 family–school collaboration action. In 2013, we officially introduced the ten major actions of new education as follows.

Action 1: Create a Campus with the Fragrance of Books

This action is designed to create a pro-reading atmosphere, integrate plentiful reading resources, launch colorful reading activities, make reading part of the daily life of teachers and students, and thus create a reading society.

It was launched because we believe books are one of the windows for us to understand history and the world. Only through books can we preserve and pass down human wisdom and civilization. Books are the fruits of human experience and lessons, invaluable spiritual treasure of mankind, an inexhaustible mine, and the cornerstone for the edifice of tomorrow. Reading is an important way of learning and a must for spiritual enhancement and inheritance. The habit of reading will bring you freedom and happiness. We firmly believe that a campus where books are not read and valued is not a school in the real sense, but just a venue for education and training. We hope this action would become the most important step for laying the spiritual foundation for our experimental schools.

Action 2: Teachers and Students Write Essays Together

This action advocates students and teachers to keep an educational diary, record educational stories and analyze educational cases, reflect on their daily educational life, and thus promote the growth of both teachers and students.

It was launched because we believe the educational diary (journal) is an important tool to provoke educators to think and innovate, and an inevitable path for the growth of critical-thinking and reflective teachers. Reading allows you to stand on the shoulders of masters while writing lifts you above your own shoulders. To have things to write about, you must take actions and make a real difference in life. Gradually, reading, thinking, and writing will become part of the daily life of teachers and students and benefit them for the rest of their lives.

Action 3: Listen to the Voice Outside the Window

This action aims to make full use of community-level educational resources, such as campus lectures and community activities, guide students to love life and foster their sense of social responsibility, and encourage the diversity of values.

It was launched to address the closed-door educational practice in many schools. A teacher who knows little about the outside world is incapable of arousing a passion for life among students or becoming the role model for them. Through this action, teachers are encouraged to follow what's happening outside the campus and respect diverse values. The Dialogue with Masters gives teachers the chance for face-to-face communication with masters and thus stimulates their desire to write. Through such activities, teachers will see the real world as it is, hear nothing but the truth, and find the true value and meaning of life and social development.

Action 4: Eloquence Training

This action takes the forms of story-telling, speech, and debate; encourages students to speak their minds; and hones their speech skills so that they will become more confident in themselves, and better at communicating with others and expressing themselves.

It was launched because we believe eloquence is important for the development of teachers and students. It is a sign of strong confidence when a person is willing and dares to speak his mind and is able to speak clearly. Self-confidence is the most important quality of a person. Without self-confidence, he won't be able to compete in the real sense. What supports your speech is your thinking. An eloquent speech is the fruit of brilliant thoughts. But the skills to communicate with others and express ourselves are exactly what are missing in our current education.

Action 5: Create the Ideal Class

This action aims to deliver a class that is equal, democratic, harmonious, and efficient, respects individuality, finds connections between book knowledge and students' life experience, and produces a resonance between knowledge, life, and living.

It was launched because we believe that class is the most important form of school education, the most important stage of a school, and the most important place for teachers and students to show themselves. School education is mainly delivered in class, and the quality of class directly determines the quality of school life and education. In a sense, education won't exist without class. That's why "Deliver the Perfect Class" is a key action of new education.

Action 6: Build a Digital Community

This action aims to build an online learning community by integrating online resources inside and outside schools so that teachers and students can learn and exchange with each other via the Internet and enhance their IT awareness and capacity.

It was launched because we believe that the IT revolution is the midwife of new education, a bridge and access to new education. Based on experimental schools and the Education Online website, we intensify efforts to integrate and apply digital learning resources, and build a digital community composed of families, schools, and communities This will enable the new education community to learn and exchange online; improve the ability of collecting, processing, and applying all sorts of information in practice; help create a learning society where lifetime learning is promoted to all members; and promote the all-around development of mankind.

Action 7: Advance One Thing per Month

This action launches one thematic campaign per month based on the mental and physical development of students and the schedule of school and social life; takes the form of thematic reading, thematic practice, outcome display, and evaluation; and tries to foster good behavior and citizenship awareness among students, and teach them things that will benefit the rest of their lives.

It was launched because we believe we should teach students things that will benefit the rest of their lives. What are these things exactly? They include good habits, such as habits of reading, thinking, compliance, planning in advance, regular exercises, and saying thank-you. Following the psychological research findings about how habits are fostered, we promote one good habit every month and spiral training throughout the primary and middle school life, to help students cultivate habits that will bring them lifelong benefits.

Action 8: Create the Ideal Classroom

This action is guided by the life narration and moral development theory, draws from the child courses, promotes the habit of reading in the morning and at noon and reflecting in the evening, and sets three goals for the teaching of all subjects so that teachers and students can create life and knowledge together and foster a unique classroom culture.

It was launched because we realize how important the classroom is for teachers and students. A dull, cold, or even violent, tyrannical classroom full of lies and a perfect, warm classroom will have entirely different effects on the life of students. A classroom is where students spend most of their youth, where they experience success and failures, sorrow and joy. To "construct the ideal classroom" is to care for each and every student on a daily basis and allow students to blossom their life in the classroom.

Action 9: Develop Excellent Curriculum

This action encourages teachers to try secondary development, integration, and innovation of textbooks while following the existing national, local, and school curricula, and turn the class into a hub of all things beautiful. It guides students to explore their experience and the inner connection between book knowledge and the world, and translate the knowledge they have learned into their own wisdom and thus fulfill their life.

It was launched because we believe courses are of special meaning for the growth of teachers and students. The more diversified and excellent the course is, the more fulfilled and achieved their life experience will be. The course should not be content with instilling knowledge into students, but should show them that knowledge is relevant and full of life wisdom. In this way it will teach students to love life and be people of virtues, good aesthetic tastes, fine feelings, wisdom, and capabilities.

Action 10: Family-School Cooperation

Through this action, the family–school cooperation mechanism is formed, the parent committee is established, and colorful activities such as the parent–child reading program are organized. It aims to involve parents more in the school life so that they can grow together with their children, and home education and school education can complement and reinforce each other and eventually realize coordinated development.

It was launched because we believe that family plays an irreplaceable role in one's development. Family–school cooperation not only means a lot for improving the quality of school education, but also is a must for the modern school system.

The above ten actions are only parts of what the New Education Experiment is doing, but they are the most urgent and important because they fill the blanks in China's current educational system. They do not have a strict theoretical system; they are carried out by following the logic of action.

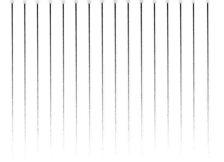

3

The New Education Experiment and Teacher Development

I. The Teacher Development Theory of the New Education Experiment
II. Case Study of Teacher Development

The New Education Experiment believes that the person speaking in front of the class determines the basic quality of education. The teacher is responsible for all class activities, course development, and other educational activities. Without the development of teachers, students' development would not be possible; without the research and development efforts made by teachers, course development would not be possible; without the practice of teachers, the ideal class would only exist like moon in the water. Teachers are the most important and fundamental force in education. That's why the New Education Experiment begins with teacher development and considers it the key to the success of the whole education process.

I. The Teacher Development Theory of the New Education Experiment

We divide teacher development into two dimensions: job identity and professional development. The former creates the inner drive for teacher development while the latter provides technical support for it. The two are complementary.

Job identity is about the teacher's ideal, passion, pursuit, and understanding of the teaching job while professional development is more closely related to one's knowledge, intellect, and skills. Together they can add great impetus to teacher development. On one hand, professional development is the basis of job identity because if you are lousy at the job, you will find it hard to truly identify with it. On the other, job identity drives professional development because if you don't identify with what you are doing and have no ideal or passion for it, it will be really difficult to achieve professional development. Professional development is about honing your skills and is down-to-earth; job identity is abstract, spiritual. It has been proved that only those who highly identify with the teaching job and are competent in doing it and passionate about it can grow into outstanding teachers and deliver high-quality education.

i. Job Identity

Martin Heidegger once suggested that your profession is essentially where your life meaning rests. In our opinion, job identity refers to the sense of belonging based on one's discovery and identity with job value. It provides strong ideological support for teachers to put their educational beliefs into action and an important path for teachers to achieve excellence.

Job identity of new education practitioners is based on the life narration theory. Life narration is the process where one sorts, reflects on, and records one's experience, growth, and value in the educational life in one's own way. Whether you realize it or not, your life is a story that keeps unfolding until the very last minute. The story is finished, and its meaning and ending fixated only when you cease to exist. Before that they are of your own choosing, and you are the only protagonist in your story.

In the new education community, we believe that every teacher is the protagonist and the author of his own life. Education is to help people examine their lives critically and write down their life stories. For a teacher, education is the main theme of his life story and takes up most of the volume, and whether he can grow into a legend and write a brilliant story out of his life is decided by whether he is truly committed to what he is doing.

Job identity comes from three sources:

First is the archetype of your life story. We compare our lives to a story, and each story is based on certain archetype, called the mirror self or the role model. Consciously or unconsciously, we all have our own archetype and we all ask the same questions: Who should I look up to? How should I spend my life? Your role model and your company will tell who you are. The influence of role models is tremendous. Therefore, new education practitioners are encouraged to look up to teachers like Confucius, Rafe Esquith, Li Zhenxi, and Li Jilin.

Second are life experiences. From the perspective of educational anthropology, all the ups and downs, conflicts and challenges we encounter in life are also great opportunities for our development. A dull, uneventful life is hardly an extraordinary one. Where challenges and conflicts lie, there are opportunities and growth. Only after withstanding and overcoming all sorts of tests and challenges can you grow into a true legend. A good teacher never shuns conflicts and challenges and always remains optimistic and upbeat in hard times. One should, as Roman Roland suggested, see the world as it is and love it. A teacher should be wise and courageous like that. He should have fundamental trust and even faith in the world, in the mankind and in himself even in the face of challenges and doubts, and instill that trust and faith into his students. Such trust and faith are the basic qualities of a teacher.

Third is the language code. As Heidegger said, "Language is the home of existence." A great legend is often written in three languages: the human language, the language of the national cultural community, and the local language of your place.

The New Education Experiment believes that thoughts about science and democracy and other outstanding fruits of human civilization should without doubt be the staple of education in our times, and that the greatest thoughts and values of mankind should be an important language we speak. But all these languages need to be translated into and conveyed by our national language, which is the metalanguage. Therefore, teachers should take the initiative to inherit and carry forward the Chinese culture and draw from its fertile soil. They should also make the most of local educational resources and enliven their class and school culture with distinct local and individual characteristics. By so doing, their teaching life will be enriched and fulfilled.

ii. Professional Development

The New Education Experiment promotes teachers' professional development in three aspects: reading, which allows teachers to stand on the shoulders of masters; writing, which elevates teachers above their own shoulders; and networking, which places teachers on the shoulders of a team. Reading is for reflection and absorption, writing for the sorting and expression of ideas, and networking for community development.

First is reading. Reading is considered the most important in the new education community. It is also the most important thing for teachers' professional development. We believe that a teacher who doesn't read won't make progress in the real sense. What's the source of educational wisdom? All the great educational thoughts in history are recorded in great books.

An essential mission of reading is to help cultivate the right mindset. Teachers should learn classic psychological theories, basic views of the educational philosophy, the best educational experience and practices, the most basic and important knowledge of the subjects they are teaching, and successful cases of teaching. The key is that they should go back to classics. Classics will show you the way to original thinking, draw your attention to fundamental issues, and inspire you to find the connections between those fundamental issues and the problems you encounter. Thus, reading classics on education and having dialogues with educational predecessors are the basis for teachers' professional development and the formation of their own educational philosophy. In doing so, teachers will become more reflective and focused on the educational life, and more resistant to the temptations of the hustling world, thus delivering better quality education.

Second is writing. If reading is for learning and absorption, then writing is the processing of thoughts. For teachers, it's not enough to stand on the shoulders of masters; they should learn to examine their educational activities critically and lift themselves above their own shoulders. The New Education Experiment encourages teachers to write about their feelings, stories, cases of education, and correspondences with students. But whatever the form, the writing should (1) reflect their true feelings and understanding; (2) be relevant to practice; (3) be objective, free of excess rhetoric; (4) engage students through the exchange of diaries, letters, and notes between teachers and students; and (5) pay attention to case studies.

Generally speaking, the writing of new education practitioners is not for fame or fortune, or for writing's own sake; it serves daily educational activities and is a basic means of self-examination and a basic approach to the happy, all-around educational life for both teachers and students.

Third is networking. We believe that it is an inevitable path for teachers, based on reading and writing, to network with other education practitioners, form a community of professional development, and seek progress together. You might walk faster on your own, but company will take you farther.

The community of new education teachers is marked by two features. First, it should have both a bottom line and a role model. The bottom line should be doable and a must for all teachers. It also needs to cultivate role models to guide the behavior of teachers. The community should be based on free will and inclusiveness. Second, it should have a common vision, which is the basis of the competitiveness, cohesion, and unity of the community. A community with a common vision will differentiate itself from others. Reading, writing, and exchange with other teachers will reshape the mental state of teachers, and such changes will serve as the best examples for others to follow.

To sum up, when a teacher works hard to build up his job identity and seek professional development, such as remaining optimistic in front of setbacks and challenges in life, intensifying efforts in reading and writing and playing an active role in the teacher community, he will surely live a brilliant educational life.

II. Case Study of Teacher Development

The New Education Experiment exerts tremendous influence on teacher development. Professor Yan Wenfan, director of the Education Leadership Department, School of Education, University of Massachusetts, Boston, in the United States, once said that the most remarkable thing about the experiment is that it bridges the ivory tower of academic research and front-line teachers of primary and middle schools, a big issue troubling the international education community. The experiment promotes teachers' job identity and professional development through "reading, writing, and living together" so that they can master educational theories and then make a real difference.

Here I would like to share the story of teacher Guo Mingxiao. Just years before her retirement, she was introduced to the new education community, which has changed her educational life and outlook completely.

Hurricanes used to have only female names worldwide. Behind the powerful alias "Hurricane from the Atlantic Ocean" is also a female. She is Guo Mingxiao, nicknamed Hurricane or Sister Hurricane, a model teacher of the New Education Experiment. Her debut was like a hurricane sweeping across the new education community. Her alias is so famous and impressive that it is used more often than her real name.

Teacher Guo started to post on the Education Online website under the alias in early 2009. She shared her experience of winter swimming in her first post, drawing a lot of admirers and followers.

But we didn't meet until the 2010 annual meeting in Qiaoxi. She was invited to share her story with new education the year before. Her speech captured the whole audience in the beginning and ended with thunderstorm applause.

Her story goes like this:

One day Guo dined out with her husband and daughter. After the meal, her husband and daughter suggested they go shopping together, but she declined and said she needed to go home now. "What do you need to go home for?" To her family's surprise, she said she needed to finish her homework for the online education program. Her daughter was amused, "Mom, you are about to retire. What do you study so hard for?" Guo became serious, "The more I learn, the more ignorant I find myself and the more urgent I feel to learn. As to retirement, if I can live until I am 80, then after I retire at the age of 55, I will still have 25 years to live. And there are so many things you can learn in 25 years." Her daughter joked, "In that case, why don't you try going to college?"

Guo replied with humor, "Don't dare me. I might take the entrance exam one day. There are people older than me taking the exam, aren't there?" Finally, her husband came out to end the conversation, "If you are happy, we are happy. I'm on your side. You should go to college."

At that meeting, Hurricane also shared the encounter with new education. It was at a meeting in Chengdu in November 2008 that her "eyes lit up" when she heard teachers from the New Education Research Center talk about the habit of reading in the morning and at noon and reflecting in the evening, and the new education child courses. Soon after the meeting, she visited the Education Online website and registered under the alias Hurricane from the Atlantic Ocean.

I don't know how she came up with this alias. Though it is just a name, the psychological effect it has should never be underestimated. Throughout history, it was common for people to draw strength by giving themselves a new name, such as Nie Er, Lu Xun, and Gai Jiaotian. Now everyone has an alias in the virtual community, and the alias also implies one's dream and expectations. I think Ms. Guo went for the alias because she wanted to draw the sweeping force from the powerful hurricane. She does live up to it with her actions, her spirit, her pursuit, and her persistence. Over the years, she has indeed grown into a hurricane sweeping across the new education community and even the Chinese education industry.

When she was a student of the New Education Online Normal School, her annual narration stood out from more than 1,000 entries submitted and was rated among the top ten annual narrations every year from 2009. In 2009, she read nearly 200 illustrated books, dozens of fairy tale books, and nearly 10 theory books. In 2010, she read classics and theory books such as *The Analects of Confucius*; *The History of Chinese Philosophy*; *The Quiet Revolution: When the Class Changes, the School Changes Too*; *The Purpose of Education*; and *Advice for Teachers*. In 2011, she continued to read extensively, lead students to read in the morning and at noon and reflect in the evening, and explore the construction of the ideal classroom while launching a class play based on fairy tales. In 2012, she delivered her own version of "Under the Sky of Lunar Calendar," pushing the lunar calendar–based new education curriculum to a new high. In 2013, months before her retirement, she developed and implemented the course "The Loneliness and Abundance of Life—The Poetry of Emily Dickinson," and directed the rehearsals of fairy tale–adapted plays such as *The Blue Bird* and *The Wings of Shadow*. In this way, she took the Online Normal School by storm every year, and among her classmates there were even college teachers.

I have read Sister Hurricane's annual narrations repeatedly and was touched every time I read. I have recommended them to my followers on Weibo. Her stories tell us that where there is a dream, there is growth. Hurricane leaves footprints wherever she travels. For more than 1,700 days of five years, she never stopped reading, thinking, or writing, never stopped "reading in the morning and at noon and reflecting in the evening," never stopped correspondence with students' parents, and never stopped swimming in winter. Each year, she would write a long article to examine herself and swim across the Jinsha River to motivate herself.

At the end of 2013, she invited me to her hometown in Yibin to give a lecture on "Live a happy, all-around educational life" to the principal and other teachers. She hoped that the seeds of new education would blossom and bear fruits in her hometown. It was around 2:00 a.m. when I rushed to Yibin from Hantai New Education Experimental School and rushed off shortly the next day after I gave the lecture. Chen Gang, principal of Renmin Road Primary School where Hurricane worked, drove me to the airport. On the way he revealed another side of Hurricane to me.

Chen was a special-grade senior teacher of math. He told me that Hurricane already launched the new education wave in the school. He said that before her encounter with new education, Hurricane was a dedicated, outstanding Chinese language teacher. She was also the teaching director of the school. Besides giving class, she had to deal with all sorts of administrative affairs every day, including arranging substitutes, listening to the lectures of young teachers, organizing teacher activities, attending conferences, presiding over research projects, and so on. She often worked until midnight.

After she joined the new education community, she shifted her attention to classroom teaching, resigned from the post of teaching director, and devoted herself to promoting new education. She took courses of the New Education Online Normal School, developed and implemented various courses, studied the ideal class, and directed plays adapted from fairy tales. She has been working hard to create the ideal classroom and growing together with her students in the process.

Principal Chen said that the magic of new education and the perseverance of Hurricane had worked together to create the most glorious chapter in her educational career and allow her and her students to "live a happy, complete education life" together.

A teacher like Hurricane is a treasure that no one would give up. In November 2013, Hurricane officially retired, but she was persuaded by principal Chen to stay in school and continue to train seed teachers and promote new education. Appreciating her practice in new education, the local educational authority hired her again and set up the Guo Mingxiao Workshop for her. She recruited five disciples from across the district and led three schools to promote new education in Cuiping district. Now, years past the retirement age, Hurricane is still as busy as before: she is leading a new education team of nearly 100 young teachers from her school and nearby schools, and she was hired as the chief lecturer of the New Education Experiment. She told us that she was still learning, which I believe. I know she is gathering new strength from learning on one hand and trying to add something new to the education scene on the other.

Sister Hurricane is an ordinary teacher with extraordinary achievements. Her educational achievements are rare but attainable as long as you are as committed as she is.

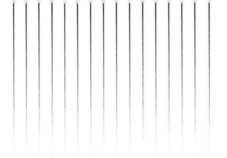

4

The New Education Experiment and Creating a Campus Full of the Fragrance of Books

In the summer of 2012, the CCTV *Reading* program hosted a campaign entitled "One of My Extracurricular Books" to look for model readers nationwide. They asked me to join the jury panel, which I declined considering many students from our experimental schools had signed up for the campaign. To my surprise, 17 out of the 30 award winners and 6 out of the 10 model readers were from New Education Experimental Schools.

Later, the production team invited me to the awards ceremony where I was introduced to a boy who was from the No. 8 Middle School of Kuitun City in Xinjiang. The director asked whether I knew who he was. I had met him before, but to my surprise, he recognized me after giving me a good look, "You are teacher Zhu, aren't you?" It turned out that this boy, named Saipuding Hasimubai, was a student in a New Education Experimental School where he saw my photos. The boy told me, "You said that one's spiritual development history was one's reading history. I will make a difference to my family and my people through reading."

---

* This case is contributed by Wang Guixiang, a good teacher of the New Education Experiment from Huahe No.1 Middle School, Shangshui County, Henan Province.

This boy was a Kazak and his class was the underdog class in his school, with classmates coming from remote rural farming areas. But his Chinese teacher, Chen Yu, made strenuous efforts to promote reading in the class: he asked parents to read together with their children, and asked students to read news summaries and write an essay per day, and read at least one self-help magazine per week and at least three classics per month.

Such reading practice has solidly prepared these students who had relied primarily on the Kazak language for daily communication for their future academic studies. Saipuding was the only finalist from Xinjiang among all the 30 finalists nationwide.

I think this story is the best anecdote about the New Education Experiment's vigorous efforts in promoting reading over the years. After more than a decade of explorations and hard work, the New Education Experiment has made reassuring progress in theoretical studies and the practice of reading.

I. The New Education Experiment's Theoretical Exploration of Reading

The New Education Experiment once proposed five key viewpoints on reading.

First, one's spiritual development history is reflected in one's reading history. If we compare one's spiritual development with one's physical development, the latter is more decided by heredity and genes while the former is less influenced by heredity or genes, but more by what one has read. Human history has seen so many spiritual monuments, and reading and thinking are the only way to get to or even surpass them. Only through reading can you enter the spiritual world of great masters such as Confucius, Mencius, and western masterminds of the Renaissance period. Without reading, spiritual growth would not be possible, nor would one achieve a complete soul. The ladder of human spirit extends forever in this way through reading.

Second, a nation's spiritual state depends to a large extent on the nation's reading level. Reading has long been considered a private behavior. This perception is partial, for it's the collective reading of a country or a nation that shapes its spiritual power, which is vital for the soft power and core competitiveness of a country. A report by the International Reading Association once pointed out that the reading capacity of a state/nation would directly shape its future. Reading plays an irreplaceable role in strengthening cultural identity and national cohesion, uplifting the national spirit, improving the qualities of citizens, purifying society, and constructing core values. For stronger spiritual power and a brighter future for us Chinese, we should attach national strategic importance to reading.

Third, a school without reading won't produce real education. Schools breastfeed students with condensed and organized human knowledge in the most efficient way of classroom teaching. But textbooks are hardly original, and a child fed only with breast milk would become malnourished. Without independent reading, without reading classics, students wouldn't go far, nor would they have a well-developed soul. The most important mission of school education is to foster students' reading habit, increase their interest in reading, and strengthen their reading capacity. A school should do more than breastfeed the students; more importantly, it should encourage independent reading so that the students can learn how to fly on their own.

Fourth, a city with the fragrance of books will surely be a beautiful spiritual homeland. In many ancient Chinese poems, the serene, regular pastoral life is depicted as the ideal life. What does a true homeland look like in neon-lit cities? It may take on a great variety of forms, but it must have strong spiritual power inside to draw people to it. The real beauty of a city is shaped by the tastes and qualities of its dwellers, and one's tastes and qualities are primarily shaped by one's reading. A brilliant city should have the most avid readers. The reading scene is the most beautiful part of urban life. A civilized city should be a learning city, habited by citizens who want to go beyond themselves and organizations that encourage people to excel, and marked by a simple, serene life and the culture of innovation. But what's most important is its learning citizens because the qualities of citizens will determine the competitiveness of a city. Only a city that promotes reading and has a favorable environment for reading can be a true spiritual homeland of urban dwellers.

Fifth, only when we read, write, and live together can we have common language, values, and vision. It's imperative to reconstruct common discourse, language, and values in schools and societies. We need to take common actions to create a shared future. But first of all, we need to have a shared history, shared heroes, shared cultural symbols, and shared spiritual food. In other words, we need to read together, have dialogue, and correspond with each other (write together) to really live together. The New Education Experiment believes that "reading, writing, and living together" is the inevitable path toward a happy, all-around educational life. It represents a cultural endeavor to restore the tradition of reading and writing. In modern society, we need to reflect on and inherit traditional culture and human civilizations; gradually form new values; reunite classes, schools, families, communities, and states; break the barriers of individualism; narrow the distance between individuals; and restore the integrity of life and interpersonal bonds, so as to create a better future.

Reading includes but is not limited to the reading of books. It can take on various forms. We can even read the lives of others to change ourselves, change the society, and then change the world. The importance of reading for individuals, schools, cities, and people can never be overestimated.

i. For the Mankind, Reading Mirrors the True Self

The New Education Experiment holds that reading is vital for one's spiritual growth. Without reading, spiritual growth and completion would not be possible. Each life is like a magic seed and each child has amazing potential that can only be awakened through reading.

Reading is the most important way toward spiritual development. The greatest wisdom and thoughts of mankind are not something you can inherit or copy from your parents, but they are hidden in the great classics. Reading plays a unique role in awakening one's true self. Books create a field where you can communicate with another soul or experience the feelings of others. Reading makes spiritual communication possible, thus enriches your spiritual world and the meaning of your life and stimulates you to pursue higher values. Reading is like a mirror from which readers and authors can see each other, and in this way, lifetime self-education becomes possible.

ii. For Education, Reading Is the Most Fundamental Means of Teaching

About two centuries ago, Victor Marie Hugo once remarked, "Books are tools to reshape one's soul." Mankind needs nutrients of enlightenment, which you can get through reading. That's why schools are so important. Schools provide the premise for the rule of books. Suhomlinski once said that when a school has nothing but books good for the spiritual growth of its teachers and students, it can still educate. We can see how much importance these two great minds attached to education and reading.

Indeed, education has gone through drastic changes in the past two centuries, and reading has appeared to be the synonym of schools, which have become the sacred temple for the worship of books. In schools, books are the most indispensable materials and the biggest asset. For the new education community, reading is the most fundamental means of teaching and a basic element found throughout the whole education and teaching process. The most important mission of school education is to help students foster the reading habit, arouse their interest in reading, and improve their reading capabilities. Only after it has achieved this mission can a school have the right to say that it has fulfilled its duties. If a person hasn't had any interest in reading or the reading habit after receiving a dozen years of schooling, he would part with books forever the minute he leaves the campus, and the education he has received would be infertile.

iii. For a Society, Reading Provides a Tool to Combat Social Inequality
Books are the best gift for promoting social equity. Through reading, the disadvantaged can improve their educational attainments, gradually grow into a well-educated group, and then change their lives. In his book *The Power of Reading*, Stephen D. Krashen observes that, though it's a fact that children from poor families have less access to books, if they are divided into two groups, then the group with more access to reading will demonstrate better language competence. This book provides a lot of data to show that a student's academic performance is closely linked to the reading environment in the school and at home, whether he has access to a library or how many libraries he has access to, the size of book collection in the library, whether his parents read or not, and how much he reads.

For a school, the hardware is the premise for education, but it's the software that determines the quality and taste of education. The key to the software quality is reading. In a peaceful reading environment, no one feels marginalized or alienated. Reading breeds a serene and rich soul and makes up for the shortage of physical matters and poverty. A school that attaches great importance to reading, even though its buildings are outdated, is perfectly capable of growing into an excellent school.

iv. For Individuals, Reading Creates the Impetus to Catch Up with Others
It has been widely agreed that reading, especially childhood reading, plays a vital role in shaping one's ambition, outlook on life, character, and life status.

The new education community argues that reading is first of all an activity involving one's consciousness, mind, cognition, and emotions; secondly, an activity that requires progressive cultivation of capacity; and last but not least, an activity through which one constructs his spiritual world and cultural life. Each individual is born different, but we can all learn to read.

Children who know how to read will be able to, based on what they have read, develop a positive outlook on life, update their attitudes toward and views of life and the world, improve themselves on all fronts, and aspire to noble purposes.

v. For Life, Reading Is a Major Avenue to a Happy Life
Psychology reveals that reading is an avenue to inner peace; it comforts the soul and gives you true happiness. When you forget yourself in reading, you will feel relaxed, peaceful, and carefree. A good book will give you the best psychological consultation. When most of the students spend most of their

time reading, school administration will be simpler and many headaches of the teachers will go away. A class in the middle of free reading will be very quiet and in good order.

Considering China's educational reality, the New Education Experiment, a non-governmental education initiative, makes reading promotion its first step to change the education scene, and the promotion of reading on campus the most important action. This is an attempt to restore the fundamental status of reading in schools, classrooms, and even families and direct educational activities back to the basics.

II. The New Education Experiment's Actions to Promote Reading

As German philosopher Johann Gottlieb Fichte declared, "Action! Action! This is what we live for." The philosophy of action is also what characterizes the New Education Experiment. The new education practitioners not only dig deep into theories, but also take the initiative to put them into practice.

i. Promote Reading on Campus

By creating a campus full of the fragrance of books, we mean to create a favorable reading environment, integrate all sorts of reading resources, organize colorful reading activities, and make reading part of the daily life of teachers and students. As Mr. Suhomlinski once said, "What makes a school is the books it has for the spiritual development of teachers and students." The meaning of reading for a school could never be overestimated. I once said that school education would not be possible without reading. It is for this reason that creating a campus full of the fragrance of books remains at the top of the New Education Experiment's list of major actions even as it expands from six to ten actions. The New Education Experiment is based on educational actions and considers reading a key foundation and a starting point for educational reform.

Many of the 3,500-plus schools of the New Education Experiment chose to create a campus full of the fragrance of books as their start project by investing heavily in building and upgrading school libraries, book squares for each grade, and book corners in each classroom. On the one hand, reading is considered the starting point of the New Education Experiment; on the other, it is one of the must-master skills for a child and a key foundation for a school to thrive. Therefore, books should be within reach in libraries, classrooms, and even passageways.

Our experimental schools have also launched colorful reading activities: the reading festival on September 28, the reading month celebrating various themes, the journey of books, the second-hand book market, the star reader competition, the reading class competition, book presentations, the writing of book reviews, stage plays and appreciation of classics adapted to films and TV series, and more.

The new education community holds that a school without a favorable environment for reading is only a training venue and that creating a campus full of the fragrance of books is the most important action to lay down the spiritual foundation for a school.

ii. Read, Write, and Live Together

At the 2007 annual meeting on new education, we proposed the idea of reading, writing, and living together. By reading together, we want to achieve mutual understanding based on education, learning, and effective dialogues. The best way to learn is through intellectual, enlightening dialogues, which can take place between teachers and students, among teachers, or among students. Learning is a process of reading, writing, and living together. Reading is a precondition and a must for such dialogues to take place, which makes reading together an ideal option for education.

The New Education Experiment stresses that parents and teachers should read together with children and that what a child reads will eventually set him apart from his peers. It calls on parents, teachers, and students to read the same book in a given period of time so that they can compare notes and share their ideas about it. Only in this way can parents and teachers truly get to know the children and avoid being strangers to each other.

In November 2011, the Parent-Child Reading Research Center (later renamed New Parents Institute) was founded to promote parent–child and teacher–student reading programs. Public-interest programs such as the Firefly Parent-Child Reading Program, the Seed Teacher Program, the New Parents School, the New Dew Special Education Reading Program, and the Fairy-Tale School, featuring parent–child reading and school–home cooperation have been organized to promote reading. More than 6,000 activities were launched in six years, involving more than eight million parents and children.

The New Education Experiment advocates not just that parents and children should read together at home, but also that teachers and students should read together at school and even teachers and administrative and logistics staff should read together at school. By reading together, parents, teachers, and students can exchange their feelings and ideas, and increase mutual understanding. This, in turn, will enhance the effect of education and school administration. In this way, every participant will be motivated to keep reading, to enjoy sharing feelings and thoughts about a book, and then acquire the intellectual capacity necessary for success in life. In this way, every participant will appreciate the true value of reading, gradually fall in love with it, foster the reading habit, and make reading an important part of his or her life.

iii. Explore the Child Curriculum to Create a Happy Childhood
The New Education Experiment has always been committed to presenting the best childhood books to our children.

For a long time, we have placed too much emphasis on the physical growth of children and too little on their spiritual growth. As a result, many children are suffering from the mismatch of their physical and spiritual growth. In reality, the secrets of childhood remain hidden and the true value of childhood books is far from being discovered. What you read in your childhood will be engraved into your heart and memory and lay down the foundation for your adult life. In other words, childhood reading will shape your future. By giving children the access to books, arousing their interest in reading, and developing the reading habit among them, we are leading them into a bigger spiritual world. We new education practitioners work hard to choose the most appropriate and beautifully written books for children, cast beautiful seeds of thought in their heart, and hope that they will blossom splendidly in their later life.

For years, we have been developing reading courses and striving to make reading not just a supplement to the Chinese language course, but an important part of subject learning and daily education. "Reading in the morning and at noon and reflection in the evening" is one of the fruits.

By "reading in the morning," we mean to start one's day by reading a poem aloud. The morning reading course is a comprehensive modern course based on the enlightening education tradition in ancient China, absorbs the techniques from Chinese and western educational schools, and is guided by advanced educational philosophy and theories and a clearly defined knowledge framework. It advocates to "make every day and every individual shine" through poem reading. In a beautiful environment created by music and arts, students read classic poems aloud together and draw inspiration and strength from these poems, which will help them cope with all sorts of temptations and pressure in life and develop a content, upbeat character.

By "reading at noon," we mean to allow students to read books appropriate for their age at noon (and at some other time in the day) every day. We believe that childhood is a colored staircase that keeps extending; it is not static. The second-graders and the fourth-graders, though kept in different classrooms steps away, are a world apart. Therefore, each grade of students should have their own readings. Based on the findings of the "Caterpillars and Butterfly" child reading project, we promote the integrated experiment of listening, reading, painting, and storytelling among the low-graders, the extensive reading experiment among medium-graders, and the collective entire-book reading experiment among high-graders. Such differentiated reading practices have demonstrated a strong therapy effect: many of the students have started to voluntarily keep a distance from TVs and games, look much fresher and more upbeat, and have better relationships with their parents and teachers.

By "reflection in the evening," we mean that students should sort out and reflect on the day after finishing the homework and write their thoughts in the form of an essay or diary. They can share their essays or diaries with teachers to get feedback or correspond with teachers to exchange thoughts. In this way, teachers and students each keep a diary of their own growth and inspire and comfort each other through writing. This has become a key part of the New Education Experiment and the daily life of participating teachers and students.

After years of experiment, the reading-oriented child course has witnessed many moving stories and inspired participating teachers, schools, and parents by showing them what a happy, all-around educational life truly is.

iv. Promote Reading Among Teachers to Stimulate Their Professional Growth

Unlike other educational experiments, the New Education Experiment considers teachers' professional growth as its starting point. Since the start of the experiment, we have launched the Education Online website. On this website, generations of young and more experienced teachers from different parts of the country have shared their experience and thoughts and achieved professional and spiritual growth, paving the way for activities of the New Education Experiment.

As to teachers' reading, the new education community agrees on the following two points. For one thing, without education-related reading, teachers won't be able to grow in the real sense. After years of exploration, the New Education Experiment has explored the "reading + writing + networking" mode for teachers' professional growth. If writing is to lift teachers above their own shoulders and networking is to allow them to stand on the shoulders of a community, then reading is to allow teachers to stand on the shoulders of great minds. For another, there exists a most reasonable knowledge structure for each specific field, professional growth will inevitably go through the process from a romantic vision to precision and then to comprehensiveness, one must go from the easy to the difficult and complicated while learning a subject, and there exists a unique reading path for each teacher. For a teacher at a certain stage of development and in a given scenario, there must be a book that best suits his or her needs. The New Education Experiment stresses the importance of "fundamental books"—classics that lay the spiritual and academic foundation for teachers and shape their mindset and thinking capacity. When teachers can truly understand such a book, it will become the source of inspiration for them while they are thinking about educational issues or reading other books on education. The New Education Experiment advocates reading for intellectual enlightenment and hopes that teachers would sort out, reflect on, and be critical about what they have read; absorb what's valuable; and internalize it into their knowledge structure, so as to enrich, optimize, or reconstruct their original knowledge structure.

The New Education Experiment has given birth to a number of teachers' communities for professional growth, such as the team of seed teachers and the online normal academy, gathering a large number of outstanding teachers cherishing the educational ideal and passion and aspiring for professional growth.

v. Develop a Recommended Reading List

We highlight the importance of reading so that people can appreciate its value and start reading; we develop reading lists in different fields and for different social groups to show people what to read. The development of such reading lists is fundamental for promoting reading, for reconstructing core values and cultural identity of the Chinese people, and for improving the nation's reading capacity. It is of strategic importance for the people, the country, and future generations.

In the late twentieth century when the New Education Experiment was just launched, I organized professors and renowned scholars to study and promote the reading list for primary and middle school students and teachers. One of the major fruits is the *New Century Education Library*, which is divided into four series dedicated to primary school students, middle school students, college students, and teachers, each series containing 100 titles (including 20 highly recommended titles). These four series of books have exerted extensive influence on campus and online nationwide and are chosen as major reference books for many primary and middle schools.

From 2006 on, we developed the "Caterpillar and Butterfly–New Education Graded Reading for Children" child book packs, which are divided into three levels—entry level, medium level, and advanced level—with 36 titles in total. This project has been widely welcomed by teachers, parents, and especially children. In August 2010, the New Reading Institute was founded, and its first undertaking was to study and develop reading lists. Since April 2011, we have released reading lists for primary school students, for preschool children, for secondary school students (including a reading list for junior middle school students and one for high school students), for entrepreneurs, for primary and middle school teachers, and for parents. We are about to release the reading list for college students and public servants as well. We have kick-started the development of reading lists by subject for primary and middle school students. In our selection of recommended books, we pay special attention to the Chinese culture and spirit and universal values conveyed by the books. For years, the New Reading Institute has provided reading lists and expert support for non-governmental organizations such as China Foundation for Poverty Alleviation, Jingxin Education Foundation, China Youth Development Foundation, and Tiantu Education Foundation.

vi. Promote Reading to Combat Cultural Poverty

We believe that reading can help people access information, gain knowledge, and soothe emotions so that people can regulate themselves, overcome difficulties, and realize their own value. Thus, promoting reading is an act of charity and an effective way to do so. It has become a new growth point in the charity sector, especially the education charity sector.

The New Education Experiment has launched a number of reading-related charity programs, including the rural education aid in West China, the "Caterpillar and Butterfly–New Education Graded Reading for Children" child book packs, the book packs for primary school students developed based on the recommended reading lists released by the New Reading Institute, mobile libraries, child book library, the Perfect Classroom library, and the Firefly Work Station. After years of operation, we have formed a mature mode for reading promotion for charity purposes, covering application by schools, public announcement and fundraising, targeted sponsorship, teacher training on reading, book donation, and the provision of classics reading courses. The Tzu Chi Foundation in Taiwan purchased 15,000 child book packs with two million yuan, bringing literary classics to hundreds of schools nationwide, including schools for children of migrant workers in Gansu, Inner Mongolia, Qinghai, Shanxi, and Beijing as well as some new education experimental schools.

Reading promotion for charity purposes is still gaining momentum among the new education community. We are working hard to bring reading to more people, especially the disadvantaged in backwaters.

vii. Strive to Make Public Reading a National Strategy

We advocate that public reading should be a national strategy, a key cultural strategy for the country and its people. Reading is an indispensable part of a nation's efforts to construct its ideological basis and core value system, and the Chinese people are no exception. Common reading is the key to the formation of a common language and common codes to the spiritual world, and an important way to construct our core value system.

Therefore, we suggest setting the national reading festival, developing the national reading program, establishing the national public reading steering committee and the national reading fund, and making public reading a national strategy, so as to effectively promote reading and build a civilized, harmonious society.

The New Reading Institute is the backbone in studying and promoting reading for charity purposes. It has been actively exploring how to promote public reading in recent years. For example, the New-Reading Lectures and reading clubs have been organized, delivering hundreds of lectures given by experts and shared reading sessions initiated by teachers and parents. The Annual Ranking of Chinese Child Books is released to guide people's choice of child books with expert opinions. The Conference of Reading Promoters we convened has become a feast for reading promoters. These efforts have not only won extensive public praise, but also helped cast the reading seeds to every corner of the society, contributing to the building of a society full of the fragrance of books.

Reading research is an endless journey; so is reading promotion. For 17 years, the New Education Experiment has been promoting reading with relentless efforts. To quote from *The Read-Aloud Handbook*, "Reading is the ultimate weapon against ignorance, poverty and despair and we need to kill them before they kill us." I believe that reading gives us wings that will take us to a wise, abundant, and happy world; it will allow us to constantly improve ourselves and aspire to our dreams.

III. Case Study

i. Teachers and Students Read Together in a Rural Classroom

I have been teaching ninth-graders in recent years, not as the head teacher but a Chinese language teacher. I believe every ordinary teacher can create the ideal classroom he wants. My school is a rural boarding junior middle school, and most of the students are from poor families. The school admits about 100 students per year, 113 at most and 99 at least.

As the lyrics of *Toward the Bright Side* go, "we must move toward the bright side, even only inch by inch." Since the fall semester of 2010, I have been trying to create my own ideal classroom with the help of new education ideas and curricula.

I name the classroom "Kaffir Lily" and put forth the slogan "Enjoy reading and write your own legend stories." I lay down the following mission for my students: to cultivate a noble, virtuous character, to discover your interest and tap your potentials through reading and activities, and to lay down a solid foundation for a complete, happy life.

To this end, we have launched many courses, such as the morning course of reading aloud Su Shi's poems, the morning course of reading about classics about cultivating a noble character, the shared reading course, the birthday course, and the course of teachers and students writing essays together.

ii. The Short Supply of Books

Teacher Zhu Yongxin once said, "One's spiritual development history is reflected in his reading history. And a nation's spiritual state depends on its reading level."

I think we should attach more importance to reading in rural primary and middle schools. Zhang Fengge, a student of mine, told me that the only extracurricular book he ever read before entering the "Kaffir Lily" class was *A Collection of Selected Compositions*. His experience was shared by many classmates. In the first few weeks of the semester, when students were asked to come forward to recommend books to the class, most of them would go for books they read in their childhood.

The ninth-graders are busy preparing for the upcoming high-school entrance exam. Moreover, most of them are children of migrant workers, separated from their parents, and tend to squander their after-school time away. For them, watching TV and playing games are obviously more fun and easier than reading. They find classics especially boring because such books are often too distant from their real life. Even if they do open a book, they just glance over page by page, without deeply considering what the book is talking about.

Meanwhile, adolescents are going through a particularly difficult period of life and are in urgent need of spiritual, moral role models to follow. By reading good biographies and novels, they can learn from the characters and develop a complete, stable personality. That's why I decided to start the shared reading program with these ninth-graders in the fall semester of 2010.

The first thing we needed was books. Many parents considered extracurricular books a waste of money. But at that time, books were not a problem for us, because in 2010, I received more than 5,000 yuan for being elected into the first batch of seed teachers of the New Education Experiment. I spent the money buying some books for myself and some books to share with my students. These shared books have been passed down class by class in these years. When the students outnumbered the books, I would use the bonus I received from the school to buy more to fill in the gap. Sometimes, students from well-off families would ask me to buy books for them so that they could write comments on the books and save them for their younger siblings.

In this way, our collection of books keeps expanding and now we have our own class library with a collection of more than 700 books. But the classroom is already crowded with students and has no room for so many books, so these books are now kept in my dormitory on campus. The red bookshelves were made with the money my students and I saved from recycling beverage bottles as volunteers for three consecutive years; the orange-red ones were made by my brother-in-law; and the iron ones were provided by the school earlier this semester.

iii. Five Steps of the Shared Reading Program

For the shared reading of each book, we take generally five steps to complete it: self-reading, role-play, discussion, extension, and internalization.

Take *The Merchant of Venice* for example. The story goes like this: in fifteenth-century Venice, merchant Antonio gets a loan from Shylock, a Jewish money lender, as a favor for his friend Bassanio who is going to propose to Portia. Shylock hates Antonio, so the loan contract provides that if the loan is not paid back in due time, one pound of flesh has to be cut off from Antonio. Bassanio's proposal is successful, but Antonio is bankrupt, has no money to pay back, and is prosecuted. To his rescue, Portia pretends to be a lawyer, wins the case, and bankrupts Shylock.

Step 1: Self-reading: To get the first impression of the story

In this step, students are free to share their feelings. Li Mengting said, "Shylock is greedy, self-interested, and cold-blooded. He is the name of devil!" Li Lidan said, "Shylock wants one pound of flesh off Antonio just for revenge. It is cruel to revenge others by hurting them physically and trying to taking their life, isn't it? We should feel for others."

Step 2: Role-play: To gain more understanding of the story

In this step, we will spend our daytime class hours (and self-study sessions at night) in a week to finish reading the book. Books like *The Merchant of Venice* may be too hard or too boring for students to read alone, for the story is too far from our current life and requires some historical background. Therefore, we spent four class hours reading aloud the book in role-plays. It was fun when everyone in the class was involved.

Step 3: Discussion: To summarize each chapter, understand characters, discuss the theme of the story, and relate it to real life

In this step, I would print a list of questions and distribute it to the class before they read the book once more. After they finish reading it a second time, the class discussion will begin. For *The Merchant of Venice*, for example, discussion questions may include the following:

1. How much do you know about the author or the historical background of the story?
2. Is it fair or cruel to cut one pound of flesh off Antonio if he fails to pay back the loan?
   A. How does Antonio treat Shylock?
   B. Is it fair for Antonio to treat Shylock like that?
   C. Is Shylock a devil or an ordinary man?
3. Is this story a tragedy or a comedy?
   A. Is this a progressive or a conservative story?
   B. Was Shakespeare an outstanding representative of Renaissance?
   C. What do you think of humanism?

    D. Portia is widely considered to be a woman of humanism. Does she treat Shylock with humanism?

    E. Self-reflection: Am I like Portia sometimes?

    F. We are after happiness, freedom, and equality, but do we truly respect the happiness, freedom, and equality of others?

4. Does Bassanio choose the right box by chance or by destiny?

    A. Is money equal to happiness?

These questions will make our reading more thought-provoking. In class discussion, we often relate what we have read to the personality development chart posted on the wall. Such discussions have obvious effects on students' personality development. For example, a student who once played Shylock used to be radical, cynical, and believed in the power of money. But after reading *The Merchant of Venice*, he had a new view about money and voluntarily donated two books to the class library. I wanted to acknowledge him before the entire class, but he declined, saying, "I didn't do this for praise. I have passed the age."

Step 4: Extension: To watch films of similar topics

In this step, we will watch some films of similar topics. For example, we watched the film of *The Merchant of Venice* after reading the novel to compare the film with the book. In the following semester, we watched films like *Exodus*, *Schindler's List*, and *La Vague*, as an extension of the shared reading program.

Step 5: Internationalization: To write essays and stage plays

I think the most memorable for each class is the participatory play. Last semester when we rehearsed the fourth act of *The Merchant of Venice*, we divided the class of more than 90 students into two groups, each rehearsing their own version. Each crew had their own director, leading actors/actresses, extras, and other staff. They really put their mind to it: some made costumes with worn scarves, some cut their hair and pasted it on their face for a mustache, some used plastic bags and cardboard to make doctorial hats, and some made coats with curtains.

After two rehearsals on weekends, on the last day of the semester, the play was staged at the end-of-semester celebration. I asked Teacher Wu to film the show and invited parents to enjoy it. The parents were all amazed by the students' amazing performance.

The play was a great success. The shared reading program changed the lives of the students and aroused their interest in learning. Their academic performance was not affected by the time they spent preparing for the play but was improved to a varying degree at the end of the semester.

iv. Change the Lives of Students Through the Shared Reading Program

I think teachers are the primary beneficiary of the shared reading program. To better explain *The Water Margin* to the class, I have read repeatedly *The Water Margin* (with commentary by Jin Shengtan) and *Commentary on the Water Margin* by Bao Pengshan, which has naturally enhanced my comprehension ability. The shared reading experience with *The Merchant of Venice* strengthened my job identity: when you make a choice, you are making a commitment and commitment itself is the biggest reward. Last semester, Liu Liang, a student of mine, wrote me a letter that concluded with the paragraph: "Thank you for what you have done. You show me what a man benefiting the entire world is like. Well you might not benefit the entire world yet, but you have certainly benefited us a lot."

After shared reading of five books in one school year, what changes do these ninth-graders have?

First, of course, is the improved reading ability and stronger interest in learning. Last semester, some students still had difficulty comprehending selected modern classics in exams, which lowered their exam scores. After taking part in the shared reading program for one semester, they have seen marked improvement in their reading and comprehension abilities. As the number of books they have read grows, students are looking for books with deeper thoughts. Many students in the class are reading books like *Sophie's World, Amusing Ourselves to Death*, and *Selected Poems of Middle and Late Tang Dynasty*, which I didn't read until 2009.

More importantly, by selecting the most appropriate classics and allowing students to have spiritual dialogue with the greatest minds in human history, the shared reading program has changed the lives of participating students.

I have a student named Zhang Haohao. When he joined the class, he felt inferior and was at a loss about studies because of some family misfortunes. But he would borrow at least one book on every weekend, and gradually he moved from the lower rank in the beginning to the top of the class at the high-school entrance exam and was admitted into the Hongzhi Class in high school. He is a brilliant high school senior now, still loves reading, and comes back to me to borrow a few books every month.

A few days ago, the municipal TV station aired his story. In the program, he said that it was the chance to play in *The Merchant of Venice* in the shared reading program that had changed his life.

I often wonder what exactly the shared reading program in this little rural classroom has brought us. I think it has enriched every individual life day by day and created life miracles through shared growth. The "Kaffir Lily" is still growing in the countryside.

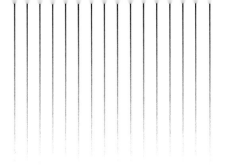

5

The New Education Experiment and Creating the Ideal Class

The classroom is the central premise for cultural inheritance, the major avenue to curriculum delivery, the nerve center of a school, and offers the key growth path for teachers and students. As the curriculum defines the main content of education, the classroom teaching shapes the main form of education. The classroom determines how the curriculum is delivered and is also an integral part of it. The way the class is organized will limit or expand the delivery of the curriculum. Then how to realize the limitless possibilities of education in the limited space of a classroom? For thousands of years, numerous educators have been trying to find the answer, as are we new education practitioners.

The New Education Experiment started the ideal class project in 2002, proposing six dimensions of an ideal class. In 2004, it announced six actions, including creating the ideal class. In 2006, it established three goals for the research of the ideal class, namely, "the effective class," "cultural diversity in the class," and "style and the individualized class." In 2008, it put forth three standards for the ideal class, and officially promoted and put into practice the framework of an effective class among experimental schools.

I. The Six Dimensions and Three Standards for the Ideal Class of the New Education Experiment
i. The Six Dimensions

In the book *The New Education Dream*, published in 2002, we propose the following six dimensions of the ideal class: engagement, affinity, freedom, integration, training intensity, and extension.

First is engagement. This means that all students in the class are effectively engaged in the whole process of education. Classroom teaching must take into account the psychological and cognitive reality of the students and on top of that effectively guide students to engage in the process. In other words, we must proceed from the common development of both teachers and students and from the cultivation of abilities for lifelong development, and guide all students to fully engage in the teaching process, so as to broaden their horizons and improve their capabilities. Among the *Resource Books for Teachers* published by Oxford University Press, there is one book titled *Learner Based Teaching*, which suggests that classroom teaching should "encourage students to help decide on the content of teaching, and try to make students' input its main content source and the center of the whole teaching activity." That is to say, cramming education without the engagement of students will never stimulate students' minds. In this sense, I suggest allocating no less than half of the class hour on average to the students for them to express their ideas and engage in other activities.

Second is affinity. This means the pleasant emotional and intellectual communication between teachers and students. Proper guidance from teachers will win respect and trust from students, arouse their interest in learning, and naturally help them foster a good thinking habit and tap their potential. In the book *Classroom Dynamics*, Jill Hadfield observed, "A class might be full of joy, friendship, cooperation, and aspiration, or silence, grudges, conflicts, and hostility." Without doubt, a class full of joy, friendship, cooperation, and aspiration will show strong affinity, which is the basis for the success of classroom teaching.

Third is freedom. This means more respect for students' choice in their way of learning. Classroom teaching should be inclusive and relaxed, guide students to relate what they have learned in class to the social context, and set their mind free. But in reality, the classroom is often run like a military camp where iron discipline is stressed and students are demanded to sit tight and stay alert, with less ease, humor, laughter, and excitement. In particular, students are required to answer questions in unison, and small talk and arguments with teachers are forbidden. Such classroom teaching will, without a doubt, check the free physical and mental growth of students.

Fourth is integration. This means the integration of knowledge of different subjects. Classroom teaching should be able to integrate all the knowledge included in the syllabus, the book knowledge with reality, and theoretical and practical knowledge with students' cognitive reality. Otherwise, knowledge is often disintegrated into meaningless fragments, such as the meaning of individual characters and phrases from a specific language context, or the singling out of an individual event from its historical background. As a result, what students receive is only dismembered knowledge, not the whole picture of it.

Fifth is training intensity. This means how much training students receive on thinking, hands-on abilities, and eloquence in class. Classroom teaching should address the needs of the times and of social development, and guide students to properly and effectively understand the connotation, nature, and methodologies of what they have learned. According to Lev Vygotsky, students learn through interaction and activities with teachers and peers by means of observation, imitation, and experience. The efficiency and effect of learning depends on how much they employ their senses in such interaction and activities. Therefore, good classroom teaching should not only be well-organized and smooth, but also allow students to practice what they have learned.

Sixth is extension. This means the extension in depth and width on top of knowledge integration and the extension of classroom teaching to social life. Classroom teaching should guide students to extend what they have learned to both ends, and understand where the knowledge comes from and how it can be applied. When you can learn from real life, apply what you have learned to it, and turn society into your classroom, your life will be enriched and blossom into more beautiful flowers, and you will expand the notion of classroom in both depth and width.

These six dimensions constitute an organic whole and cover nearly all the variables related to the implementation of the ideal class. Behind each dimension lies a keyword of the ideal class, and these dimensions are mutually dependable and irreplaceable.

Engagement – key participants
Affinity – emotional attachment
Freedom – educational ecology
Integration – knowledge
Training intensity – practice
Extension – life

It thus can be seen that these dimensions are proposed mainly to evaluate classroom teaching from the students' perspective.

ii. The Three Standards

The New Education Experiment established three standards for the ideal class in 2008: implementing the framework for effective teaching; discovering the inner beauty and greatness of knowledge; and finding deep resonance among knowledge, social life, and the individual life of teachers and students. They provide us with the teachers' perspective to reflect on classroom teaching.

Of these three standards, the first one is of particular importance and deserves detailed analysis and explanation. It is about how to lay a solid foundation for classroom teaching and truly implement the framework for effective teaching. This standard is raised to guarantee the efficiency and the basic effect of classroom teaching.

The framework for teaching is a tool that helps teachers understand and discipline the class and achieve their teaching goals. As Charlotte Danielson remarked, it serves as a roadmap for new teachers to navigate them through the first lost days of teaching, and a support stand for experienced teachers to improve their teaching efficiency. It can not only regulate teaching behavior, but also help us better observe and evaluate classroom teaching.

Educators have been struggling to find such a framework for teaching that really works. More than 200 years ago, J. F. Herbart and his followers Tuiskon Ziller and Wilhelm Rein divided the teaching process into five steps: preparation, presentation, association, generalization, and application, which were rephrased and expanded into six steps by N. A. Kaiipob in his book *Pedagogy*. Later behaviorist B. F. Skinner, cognitivists J. S. Bruner and R. M. Gagne, and humanist Carl Ransom Rogers all conducted systematic analysis on the framework and process of teaching from different angles. In 1996, Charlotte Danielson published the book *Enhancing Professional Practice: A Framework for Teaching*, which proposes a framework for teaching that contains 66 elements, 22 components in four sections.

In his book *Effective Teaching Methods*, Gary D. Borich explains the "backbone structure" of effective classroom teaching as follows. It should (1) attract students' attention and arouse their curiosity with all sorts of teaching materials including graphics, images, proportional models, and films; (2) inform learners of the teaching goals; (3) stimulate students to recall related knowledge they have mastered; (4) present stimulating materials; (5) trigger expectation; (6) provide feedback; and (7) evaluate the behavior.

Of course Chinese scholars in pedagogy have made their contributions in this regard.

Qiu Xuehua advocates trial teaching and divides the teaching process into seven steps: preparing for exercise, demonstrating trial questions, self-directed learning of the text, trial exercise, group discussion among students, instruction from the teacher, and the second trial exercise. He emphasizes trial and exercise by students before instructions from the teacher.

Former professor Lu Zhongheng from the Institute of Psychology of Chinese Academy of Sciences proposes a tutoring mode for self-directed learning, asking teachers to spend 15 minutes before the start and the end of the class to enlighten the students and summarize the class, and leave the rest of the time to students for reading, doing exercises, and collecting feedback on their own.

Yangsi Middle School in Taixing, Jiangsu Province, has put forth a framework featuring "learning before teaching and in-class exercise." It consists of three parts: learning, teaching, and exercise. The self-directed learning process contains the following steps.

1. Specifying teaching goals
   The teacher explains the teaching goals with the help of a projector (orally or writing them down on the blackboard) and motivates students to learn (about one minute).
2. Specifying requirements for self-directed learning
   The teacher explains the content, duration, and methods of self-directed learning and how to evaluate the learning effect (about two minutes).
3. Self-directed learning
   The teacher moves around the classroom to find out what problems students have in learning (five to eight minutes).
4. Grasping learning outcomes
   Students make presentations and take exercises from which the teacher can understand what questions and confusion they have and prepare for teaching accordingly (five to eight minutes).

Self-directed learning is followed by teaching: instructions will be given regarding common questions the students have. Then group discussions will be organized to field these questions (eight to ten minutes). The class will end with in-class exercises taken by students and comments from the teacher (15 minutes).

Based on the teaching mode of Yangsi Middle School, Dulangkou Middle School in Shandong Province has developed its own mode of self-directed learning. It includes three modules—preparation, presentation, and feedback—and six links—exchange during preparation, goal establishment, group collaboration, presentation improvement, consolidation, and assessment.

While doing an experiment to massively improve the math teaching effect in Qingpu County, Shanghai, Mr. Gu Lingyuan also proposed an effective structure for classroom teaching, including question-based scenario (question-based teaching), trial instructions (guiding students in exploration, discovery, and application while giving instructions), variant exercise (organizing graded variant exercises), systematic summarization (guiding students to continuously construct the knowledge system), and feedback and adjustment.

Drawing experience from predecessors, the New Education Experiment has formed its own framework for effective classroom teaching based on the philosophy and ideas of new education. This framework contains the following five parts:

1. Understanding of the textbooks and the students
   This is part of the class preparation required for the teacher.
2. Establishing teaching goals
   Teaching goals can be divided into fundamental, supporting goals, the fulfillment of which leads us to higher goals; core goals, which reflect the key content of classroom teaching; affiliated and extended goals, which are associated with thoughts, emotions, and values; and individualized goals for different students.
3. Goal-oriented homework for self-directed learning
   Students' self-directed learning before a class should make the most of their initiative to address all teaching goals.
4. Clearly defined teaching modules
   Classroom teaching is required to be divided into several modules, each with specified goals and duration, so that every minute in class will count and be well spent at a necessary pace and in diversified forms. Meanwhile, the teacher should develop individualized lists of self-directed learning for students to truly serve students' learning needs and make self-directed learning the heart of classroom teaching. Generally, the teaching content is placed in the left column and students' self-directed learning in the right column.
5. Reflection
   This framework basically inherits the traditional teaching process of "goal and strategy evaluation," with two novelties: for one thing, it places particular emphasis on the leading role of specific targets; for another, the independent learning of students is guaranteed throughout the whole framework starting from class preparation.

Every teaching framework is rigid and complicated in its own way. At first, many teachers found it hard to adapt to the effective teaching framework proposed by the New Education Experiment, from establishing goals, to designing the teaching strategy and developing the learning list. Like other teaching frameworks, however, the New Education Experiment's teaching framework is designed to guarantee the efficiency and basic effect of teaching. Once implemented smoothly, it will help the teacher keep the class in good order and significantly improve teaching efficiency. Qu Liangxia, a teacher from Anyu

Primary School in Jiangxian County, Shanxi Province, once said, "There were hard times. When I started to prepare with this framework, I found it hard to understand and operate. But gradually what's confusing and vague became clear. It was a process of self-improvement. In fact, this framework has improved my teaching effect. I really think I should have used it earlier."

According to the second standard, the ideal class should be able to discover the inner beauty and greatness of knowledge. This standard is marked by quality dialogues.

If the first standard is about rules and norms, then the second and third standards are more about freedom. The first standard is based on the textbooks, or the first syllabus as in the words of Suhomlinski, while the second standard is centered on the text, or the second syllabus.

"Knowledge" here refers not to knowledge contained in textbooks, but that outside them; not static, fragmented knowledge, but dynamic and integrated knowledge in different contexts. Also, by "discovering" we mean the whole process from raising to answering questions, including exploration and representation based on the exploration results, the methods, and the direction of exploration.

The greatest beauty of knowledge lies in that it intellectually appeals to and challenges teachers and students and that guided, accompanied, assisted, and supervised by teachers, students follow patterns to explore the unknown, and acquire skills and the methods of learning. The core of the beauty is intellectual challenge and training.

It thus can be seen that to discover the greatness and inner beauty of knowledge is to effect in-depth dialogues between teachers, students, and the texts in the teaching process. Such a dialogue can take place between the person and knowledge (represented by the world and the texts) and between the person and others (represented by teachers, other students, and other readers).

In this process, students are not containers passively receiving knowledge; instead their interest and curiosity will be aroused, they will take the initiative to do exploratory learning, experience and feel the setbacks and joys of knowledge learning and discovery so that their potential can be fully tapped and the teaching effect improved. Meanwhile, teachers will no longer act as some middleman between students and knowledge, or simply pass the knowledge to students; instead they will act as a bridge between the knowledge and students, narrow the gap precisely whenever they are needed, or even explore the path of "question – knowledge – truth" together with students and grow with them.

According to the third standard, the ideal class should be able to arouse deep resonance between knowledge, social life, and the individual life of teachers and students. This standard is marked by individuality.

If the first and second standards are more about knowledge, the third standard is more closely related to life. To meet this standard, knowledge should not be a dead system, but a living existence, a vehicle to guide teachers and students to explore and interpret the truth of life and evoke great sympathy among them before it is internalized into their individual life abilities. Each class should be unique from others, customized to every single student in it. It should allow each and every individual in it to grow and have a unique experience. The sympathy it evokes among teachers and students should be an individualized yet shared feeling produced by the encounter of greatness.

The ideal class meeting this standard will translate knowledge acquisition into life enrichment, which is realized by review and reflection after the acquisition of knowledge and skills. Then classroom teaching will go beyond the representation of knowledge and related background information, stimulate the growth of individual life, and achieve a higher end. As Karl Theodor Jaspers once remarked, "Education is an art to guide people to look back for the epiphany moment."

This is the natural result of theoretical development of classroom teaching. While Herbart stressed the learning of knowledge and John Dewey advocated the importance of social life in classroom teaching, the post-modern classroom teaching theory places more emphasis on the life experience of every participant. The New Education Experiment holds that these three schools should not be considered separately but should be viewed a complete whole. Their common ground will be eventually reflected in teachers and students.

These six dimensions and three standards together wave out the ideal class in the eyes of new education practitioners: full of vitality, fun, and wisdom.

Of course, education research is an endless journey and the ideal of education can always go higher. In October 2016, Vice President Tong Xixi of the New Education Institute raised four standards for the ideal class: first, constructing the cognitive structure for basic knowledge; second, discovering the inner beauty of knowledge; third, arousing resonance between knowledge, real life, and individuals; and fourth, applying knowledge to practice. In practice and in theory, we are still working hard to create our own ideal class.

II. The Ideal Class and the Ten Major Actions of the New Education Experiment

The New Education Experiment is an experiment of action. We have been trying to develop new theories, test existing theories, and integrate different theories through actions. In the past 17 years, we have identified the following ten major actions based on experience summarization and accumulation: "Create a Campus with the Fragrance of Books," "Teachers and Students

Write Essays Together," "Listen to the Voice Outside the Window," "Eloquence Training," "Construct the Ideal Classroom," "Build a Digital Community," "One Thing per Month," "Create the Ideal Class," "Develop Excellent Curriculum," and "Home–School Cooperation."

The "Create the Ideal Class" action is closely linked to the other nine actions.

To create the ideal class, teachers and students, parents and their children need to read together to expand their knowledge background.

To create the ideal class, teachers and students need to write essays together so that they can reflect on the teaching process and make constant progress.

To create the ideal class, educators need to listen to the voice outside the window, from outside the educational sector, to draw inspiration.

To create the ideal class, we need to train students on eloquence and the ability to express their ideas and communicate with others so that they can find deeper sympathy with others.

To create the ideal class, we need to build a digital community, a scientific, open, and vast platform that follows the latest developments in the world.

To create the ideal class, we need to advance the one-thing-per-month program so as to help students translate the skills they have acquired into a habit.

To create the ideal class, we need to develop excellent curriculum because the classroom is where the curriculum is executed, and without excellent curriculum, there won't be ideal textbooks for the class.

To create the ideal class, parents and schools need to work together to multiply the effect of education through multitiered interaction of stakeholders.

But now I would like to spend more time elaborating the ideal class's relationship with teachers' growth and the ideal classroom.

The efforts to create the ideal class are most directly associated with teachers' growth. The quality of the teacher will decide the quality of teaching and the class. According to *Instruction: A Models Approach* written by Mary Alice Günter et al., a good teacher should be able to regulate the class, create a pleasant psychological environment for learning, properly handle interpersonal relations, and motivate students to study and aspire for higher, better ends. A good teacher should also be a good learner, able to achieve the teaching goals with students, find out why the teaching plan fails, make the teaching process interesting, give students the opportunity to access information and practice, and teach students what and why.

Each educational reform has its own focus and logical basis. The new curriculum reform aims to change the educational scene by changing the curriculum and the new basic education experiment advocates injecting life into the class. The New Education Experiment bases everything else on teachers' growth because it believes that it is the teacher who educates, and the quality of the teacher will decide the quality of the class and curriculum. An outstanding teacher will be able to develop an excellent curriculum and naturally inject vitality into the class.

Each of the three standards for the ideal classroom is directly related to teachers' quality. The higher the standard, the higher the demand is on teachers' quality. Comparatively speaking, the first standard is rolled out as a requirement for new and young teachers, with the attempt to regulate their teaching behavior, and guarantee basic teaching quality and the fulfillment of basic teaching goals with the help of an effective teaching framework. In other words, it introduces the framework structure and the bottom line into the originally chaotic teaching process. This is also the secret to the successful reform of Yangsi Middle School and Dulangkou Middle School. But to meet the second and third standards, it will be hard to regulate and limit teachers' behavior with any mode or structure; it is up to the teachers' quality, sense of responsibility, reading experience, reflection, teamwork spirit, and so on. In fact, only when a teacher can shake off rigid rules and develop a unique teaching style can he or she deliver a truly unique class that allows every individual student to blossom.

Creating the ideal classroom is also closely related to delivering the ideal class.

To create the ideal classroom is to create an individual classroom culture under the guidance of the life narration and moral cultivation theory of the New Education Experiment. To do so, teachers and students should draw strength from the child curriculum of the New Education Experiment, "read in the morning and at noon and reflect in the evening," strive to meet the three standards of the ideal class, and make progress together. To create the ideal classroom is to allow each individual in it to grow into someone who is virtuous, sympathetic, and knowledgeable; has a strong personality and good aesthetic taste; and is well-trained for coordinated development in all respects. Gradually students will acquire abundant knowledge and experience and relate them to new knowledge so as to better understand and apply the new knowledge and amplify the learning effect.

Therefore, the ideal class of the New Education Experiment requires both teachers who have received training in writing, reading, and professional networking from the New Education Experiment and students who have acquired enough knowledge and intellectual capacity from the new education child curriculum and efforts to create the ideal class. The framework for teaching can guarantee the basic effect of classroom teaching, but a good teacher should never depend completely on the framework or any technique in teaching; otherwise, he would only instill knowledge and skills into students, instead of shaping them into happy, complete human beings. This is why the New Education

Experiment values but is not limited to the effective teaching framework. The ideal class is hard to create because it takes sustained concerted efforts from both teachers and students, and can never be truly replicated because it bears the signature mark and style of its teachers and students.

A classroom is like a carrying pole, with the curriculum at one end and individual life at the other. It is a space where teachers and students gather for a specific period of time to discuss the teaching content.

To the end, teachers and students are still the core to the efforts for creating the ideal classroom, developing excellent curriculum, and delivering the ideal class, as well as other actions of the New Education Experiment. All educational activities are for and by teachers and students. To create a happy, all-around educational life is the ultimate goal of the experiment's ideal classroom.

III. Create the Ideal Class: A Case Study

Below is the implementation plan for constructing the ideal classroom by an experimental school in Haimen. There are some differences in the line of thinking from the New Education Experiment, but they are the result of creativity and initiative of the experimental school and of great reference value.

i. Guiding Principles

A major guiding principle is following the Scientific Outlook on Development, the new education philosophy, and instructions of the Municipal Education Bureau including Guiding Opinions on Intensifying Efforts to Create the Ideal Class. Additional guiding ideologies include reforming classroom teaching with the course navigation teaching paradigm, building a favorable environment for teaching research, and guiding teachers to explore the way to create the ideal class based on classroom teaching research; allowing students to master their own learning process; and improving the benefits of classroom teaching and the teaching capacity and research capacity of teachers.

ii. Theoretical Basis

1. The core idea of the New Education Experiment

   The core idea of the New Education Experiment is for all people and for all aspects of people's lives. The experiment calls on us to have absolute faith in the potential of teachers and students; teach things that will be useful for the rest of students' lives; value students' mental status and advocate the experience of success; stress individuality and specialty education; and allow teachers and students to have dialogue with the noble human spirit. The experiment strives to create a paradise for students, an ideal stage for the professional development of teachers, an ideal platform for schools to improve educational quality, and an ideal spiritual homeland for the new education community.

2. Create the ideal class

The ideal class should be equal, democratic, safe, and enjoyable. It should not be oriented toward knowledge or subjects, but to students' development. It should truly integrate knowledge, capabilities, and attitudes; teach students in accordance with their aptitude; and be relevant to the real life of students and teachers. It is evaluated by the following six indicators: (1) engagement—the voluntary and active participation of students; (2) affinity—equal cooperation and communication between teachers and students; (3) freedom—a relaxed, harmonious, and natural environment; (4) integration—the integration of knowledge, methods, capabilities, and goals; (5) training intensity— experience and practice; and (6) extension—relevance to social life. It has three standards: (1) implementing the effective teaching framework and laying a solid foundation for classroom teaching; (2) discovering the greatness and inner beauty of knowledge; and (3) arousing profound resonance between knowledge, social life, and the individual life of teachers and students. It should also be authentic, exciting, and effective.

3. Adapt the curriculum to the aptitude of students through classroom teaching reform

Teachers should teach according to the aptitude of students and engage all students in teaching activities, especially those who show little interest in classroom teaching. Teaching should be in the service of learning. Teachers should guide students in exploratory learning on their own or through teamwork, allow students to do self-directed learning before teaching, and adapt the teaching content to the learning progress of students. The teaching should be concise, leaving enough time to students to do exercises. Teachers should provide clues to challenging questions. In each class, no less than 15 minutes should be reserved for students' self-directed learning, exercises, corrections, and thinking to better motivate them.

iii. Implementation Goals

1. To specify the six basic modules of classroom teaching

To make the basic modules of "goal statement, task/scenario specification, self-directed learning, collaborative and exploratory learning, presentation and guidance, and test and reflection" more operable, highlight the importance of self-directed learning, presentation, and teamwork modules; guide teachers to respond quickly to students' needs; fundamentally change teaching and learning behavior; and construct the classroom teaching mode that suits the school's conditions and reflects the guiding principles of the new curriculum.

2. By studying and constructing the ideal class teaching mode, to make the classroom a paradise for students' self-directed learning, "allow every student to master his own learning process," and promote the professional growth of teachers.

3. To specify the assessment criteria for classroom teaching in six aspects
   The classroom teaching effect should be assessed in the following six aspects: engagement, affinity, integration, freedom, training intensity, and extension.

iv. Basic Teaching Modules

1. Three basic links: self-directed learning, presentation, and test
   Self-directed learning: to understand the goal, the task, and the method
   Presentation: to present the problem, the solution, and the effect
   Test: to make sure students meet the basic requirements, improve their abilities, and extend learning

2. Basic modules for class preparation: three-dimensional goals, teaching resources, course planning, navigation strategy, homework design, and adjustment and reflection

   A. Three-dimensional goals
      Goals should be set according to students' learning progress, the textbooks, and the curriculum standards. "Knowledge and skill" goals should be stated in a concise, straightforward, and clear way so that teachers know what knowledge and skills students should master. Goals about "the process, methods, emotions, attitudes, and values" should be based on the fulfillment of knowledge and skill goals and avoid being reduced to lip service.

   B. Teaching resources
      Teaching resources generally include the learning and life experience of students, relevant background information, teaching and learning supplies, methods to identify key knowledge, strategies to overcome learning challenges, and so on. Learning resources should be developed based on students' learning progress.

   C. Course planning
      Course planning covers the content, methods, process, results, and duration of learning. While planning, teachers should step into the shoes of students, respect the cognitive pattern of students, scientifically design homework and the task list for classroom teaching, specify tasks and learning methods in the design, and advocate self-directed, collaborative, and exploratory learning.

   D. Navigation strategy
      The navigation strategy refers to the learning content, methods, and means teachers design catering to the learning progress of students. It should take into account students' learning progress and focus on

arousing students' learning interest, guiding exploratory learning, inspiring students, organizing in-class exercises, and so on.

E. Homework design

This module includes the design of in-class exercises and after-school homework and should integrate and optimize teaching resources. It should be differentiated and graded to cater to the different needs and levels of students.

F. Adjustment and reflection

This module includes the reflection on the experience and lessons drawn from the teaching process as well as adjustments made accordingly so as to assess and optimize the teaching process. Adjustment and reflection should be made in a timely and effective manner.

3. Basic modules of classroom teaching: goal statement, task specification, self-directed learning, collaborative and exploratory learning, presentation and guidance, and test and reflection

A. Goal statement

The goals of classroom teaching should be stated in a scientific, concise, and assessable way. The goal statement is to help teachers and students understand the direction of teaching and learning and navigate the whole course.

B. Task specification

It is important to translate the learning goals into specific tasks and make them attainable. The tasks should be specific in content and purpose, graded, and scenario-based. The purpose is to motivate students, fully engage them in learning, and challenge them intellectually.

C. Self-directed learning

This is an independent learning process in which the basic learning tasks are finished. The purpose is to dig up the learning potentials of students, improve their ability of self-directed learning, and help them foster a good learning habit, raise questions, and build up the knowledge base before teaching. Teachers should create a favorable environment for self-directed learning, understand the learning progress of each student, and provide guidance when necessary.

D. Collaborative and exploratory learning

This is a collective learning process in which higher-level learning tasks are accomplished. The purpose is to solve problems encountered in self-directed learning, explore certain themes, exchange learning outcomes, improve students' ability to learn on their own or with others, make sure every student meets the basic learning goals, and prepare them for presentation. It may take forms such as group learning and interaction between students or between students and teachers. Teachers should keep an eye on the class progress, guide group study, and help those in need when necessary.

E. Presentation and guidance

This is a teacher–student interaction process to meet the learning goals and take learning a step higher. The purpose is to exchange and share learning outcomes, inspire each other, and enrich the emotional experience of learning. It includes presentations within groups and before the whole class. Teachers should watch out for useful teaching information, offer proper clues or guidance when necessary, and extract and refine the key points.

F. Test and reflection

This module is to test and reflect on the preestablished learning goals. The purpose is to consolidate the learning outcomes, identify problems, and find remedies in a timely manner. The test should correspond to the learning goals, focus on key problems, and be graded in content.

Reflection is an indispensable part of every module. Teachers should guide students to reflect on the learning process, summarize experience and methods, and think about problems they have in every module. After learning something new, students should relate it to the learning goals specified before class begins, especially to what they have learned before, so as to foster the consciousness and ability to integrate knowledge.

The teaching of artistic and sports subjects should proceed from the subject characteristics and follow the core principle of Course Navigation. Suitable modules for class preparation and classroom teaching should also be developed to advance the teaching reform for these subjects.

v. Implementation Principles of the Course Navigation Teaching Paradigm

1. Students first

Students are the masters of the learning process. Teaching should be in the service of learning. Classroom teaching should be student-oriented and enjoyable for students. Teachers should lead students to questions and then answers and shift the focus of education from teaching to learning.

2. Learning before teaching

This is to highlight the important role of students in classroom teaching. Teachers should encourage students to conduct collaborative and exploratory learning first so that the ensuing teaching can be more relevant, inspiring, and directive for them. Teachers and students are expected to learn from each other by exchanging ideas in class.

3. Student-oriented teaching

   Teachers should determine the proper goal, content, and method according to students' learning progress, needs, and will; align their teaching with students' learning process; and respect students' psychological and cognitive characteristics in teaching.

4. Guidance

   Teachers should adapt the teaching approach and method to the learning progress and outcome of students, actively create scenarios to arouse students' curiosity, and guide students to learn on their own, enjoy the learning process, and go beyond the preestablished teaching plan.

5. Teaching–learning interaction

   Teachers and students should collaborate and interact with each other by means of engagement and exchange in the process of implementing learning tasks. The purpose is to keep students interested, passionate, and active throughout the learning process and make the class dynamic and intellectually challenging.

vi. Requirements for Promoting the Course Navigation Teaching Paradigm

1. Module-based teaching

   When the paradigm is first implemented, its philosophy and basic modules should be strictly observed.

2. Student-oriented class preparation

   The priority should be shifted from teaching to learning. Before each class, teachers should develop a teaching plan suitable for students, clearly stated preparation assignments, and a list of learning tasks.

3. Learning before teaching

   Each class must dedicate some time to the self-directed learning of students under the guidance of teachers. Then teaching will proceed according to the learning outcomes.

4. More time on learning than on teaching

   In each class, at least two-thirds of the time should be allocated to the learning and exercise of students, leaving no more than one-third of the time for teaching.

5. Teacher–student interaction

   The teacher–student interaction should not go one-way, but two-way so that teachers and students can learn from each other and grow together.

6. In-class exercise

   In each class, students should have no less than 15 minutes to do exercises to check their learning outcomes.

7. Reflection on the teaching process

   Teachers should reflect on the teaching process in a timely manner, make the best of in-class resources, and make corrections immediately if any teaching error is made. Teachers must draw on the experience and lessons and think about areas to be improved after each class.

8. Emotional support

   Teachers should take the initiative to understand what problems students encounter in the learning process before each class, not afterward; encourage and guide them to solve these problems; consolidate their learning basis; allow every student to really benefit from the learning process; kindle their passion for learning; and tap their learning potential.

vii. Specific Measures

1. Strengthening theoretical training for teachers

   A. To strengthen school-based training and promote the new education community's outlook on the class, teaching, students, assessment, and values

      The focus should be placed on the study of the *Guiding Opinions on Intensifying Efforts to Create the Ideal Class* and the *Operational Guide to the Teaching Paradigm* for each subject, as well as the study of theories and practices of the ideal class, so as to help teachers change their teaching mindset and adapt their outlook on the class, teaching, students, assessment, and values to the New Education Experiment. School-based training should take a variety of forms, and combine theoretical study with practice, self-directed learning with collective study, and open lectures with group discussion, observation, and exchange, to better prepare teachers for the promotion of the New Education Experiment.

   B. To advance school-based research that targets specific problems and is based on the analysis of teaching cases and behavioral research

      The basic research process goes like this: identify problems – establish the team – study relevant theories – discuss teaching cases – improve the behavior – identify more problems. Then another round of research begins. Specifically, it includes two stages and five links. The first stage includes three links: study – class preparation, trial teaching – class observation, discussion – improvement; and the second stage, two links: teaching again – class observation again and discussion – reflection. School-based research is aimed to improve teachers' teaching practice and reflection and is a prerequisite for the creation of the ideal class.

Teachers should actively take part in training programs organized by the municipal teachers' training center, to reflect on their teaching experience and improve their skills through case study and group discussion. Such training programs should be provided on a regular basis to cover all the teachers in the city.

2. Reforming the classroom teaching evaluation system

    Classrooms should implement the *Ideal Class Teaching and Evaluation Framework* and the *Table of Quantified Assessment of Classroom Teaching under the Course Navigation Teaching Paradigm in Haimen City* and advance the reform through assessment (see Tables 5.1 and 5.2).

3. Strengthening collective class preparation

    A. After the third class in the afternoon on Wednesday every two weeks, each member of the class preparation group shall bring his own teaching plan to join the school-organized collective class preparation program. Teachers will share their understanding of the teaching content, teaching design, methods, and so on, especially how to help students understand key and difficult points. They will also discuss their estimation of problems students might have or how much of the content students can master.

    B. One member of the class preparation group gives an open class (in rotation within the group), while the rest of the group observes to see how the teacher explains the key and difficult points, how students react in class, how much of the content students master, and how much of the collective class preparation result is reflected in class. After class, the lecturer shall reflect on the classroom teaching experience, summarize its experience and lessons, and specify areas for improvement; then observer teachers shall speak their mind, identify merits and shortcomings, offer suggestions for improvement, and reflect on their own teaching experience.

    C. Guidance and supervision. The staff of the teaching affairs department shall attend each collective class preparation session to listen to the voice of teachers and offer guidance. They shall also actively take part in class observation, review, and reflection with other teachers. Each class preparation group shall make a monthly presentation on their activities, which will be scored by teachers in the school (with the full score of 10 points), and the average of four scores will be calculated in the performance assessment of teachers with the weight of 20 percent.

4. Strengthening research on teaching practice

    The classroom teaching survey shall be conducted on a regular basis in order to advance the curriculum reform and improve teaching quality. The school leadership shall visit the classroom often, organize the middle management and core teachers to launch teaching survey and assessment activities, comprehensively understand the current status of classroom teaching, probe into factors influencing the effect of classroom teaching, summarize experience, identify problems, advance the curriculum reform, and improve teaching quality.

TABLE 5.1 Ideal Class Teaching and Evaluation Framework

Teaching module		Teaching elements
Teaching goal	Determining the basis for the setting of teaching goals	Understand and state relevant requirements put forth in the curriculum standard
		Understand and state the requirements of the textbook and the teaching unit concerned
		Test and state students' original understanding about the knowledge or theme in question
	Evaluation against teaching goals	Is the statement clear, specific, and unambiguous?
		The correctness of the teaching content
		The breakdown and integration of the three-dimensional goals
		Is it balanced and flexible?
The teaching strategy	Key points of the teaching strategy	Selecting and appropriately integrating teaching resources in the teaching process
		Design the specific teaching links and process
		Design the list of learning tasks for students
	Assessment of the teaching strategy	Is most of the class hour spent on fulfilling key goals?
		Is there any link unnecessary?
		Did the teacher inspire students in a clever, effective way?
		The teaching strategy is flexible and has variations. Its adaptation to the actual classroom teaching process
Teaching management	Quantified contents for class management	Student engagement and the coverage and amount of exercise
		Class discipline
		The management of study groups and individual tutoring for specific students
		Was the class delivered in a correct, concise, clear, and passionate manner?
	Qualified contents for class management	Was the class going on smoothly, with clear and rich content?
		Were class interaction and dialogue effective, equal, safe, and inspirational?
		The mood and curiosity of students
Teaching assessment	Random assessment of classroom teaching	Instant feedback on students' behavior such as expressing themselves in class
		Instant comments on students' mood and learning attitude
	Homework design assessment	Did the teaching behavior match the teaching goals?
		Did the classroom teaching generate real cognitive conflicts to stimulate learning in the real sense?
		Was the classroom teaching correct, balanced, tiered, and diversified?

TABLE 5.2 Table of Quantified Assessment of Classroom Teaching under the Course Navigation Teaching Paradigm in Haimen City

Teacher:	Teaching content:	Class:	MM/DD:	Score:		
School	Name		Subject			
Class-1 indicators	Class-2 indicators				Value	Score
Engagement	The whole class: The engagement rate is 100%.				20	
	The whole process: Students engage in the whole process ranging from reading, speaking, discussion, comments, to reflection. No less than two-thirds of the class hour are spent on self-directed learning and collaborative, exploratory learning.					
	Effectiveness: Students are actively and seriously engaged, with great enthusiasm and concentration. They have met the requirements in aspects of knowledge and skill acquisition as well as the learning process, methods, and skills.					
Affinity	Teacher–student relations: The teacher is amiable and sincere. The teaching content is delivered lively and fluently and with passion. Students' personality and dignity are respected. Information exchange and emotional communication go two-way.				15	
	Organizational status: The learning activities are reasonably organized, and the teaching process well designed and controlled in a lively atmosphere. Students have passion for learning and good learning habits.					
Freedom	Time and space: Students have the time and space for thinking and the freedom to choose to do certain tasks. There is full interaction among students, and between teachers and students.				15	
	Learning situation: Students are active in thinking and can raise questions. Teachers and students can learn from each other and make progress together.					
Integration	Three-dimensional goals: Goals promote the all-around development of students and attached great importance to the process of knowledge acquisition and the mastering of learning methods.				20	

Category	Weight	Content
		Teaching content: The content of textbooks is employed creatively, the content of in-class exercises well integrated to suit the needs of students and highlight key points. The teaching content is arranged in a logical, tiered way, with a focus on helping students master basic knowledge and skills, develop basic ideas, and accumulate basic experience.
		Methods: Including learning before teaching, student-oriented teaching, in-class exercises, and self-directed, collaborative, and exploratory learning
Exercise	20	Time for exercise: No less than one-third of the class hour; in-class exercise is a must.
		Content of exercise: It should be elementary, well-targeted, and tiered.
		Effect of exercise: The expected goal is reached, the pass rate is high, and some students have met the goal for extended learning.
Extension	10	Generative teaching: The teacher is adaptive, keeps the class under control with flexibility, and knows when to give guidance for specific problems and how to inspire students to think out of the box at certain points.
		Student development: Students are able to build their own knowledge system based on what they have learned, are good at making comments, dare to speak their mind, and have their individuality fully respected.
Note		Any of the following situations will result in a failure: 1. The principle of "learning before teaching and student-oriented teaching" is not observed. 2. The lecture exceeds 15 minutes. 3. The content of class preparation is irrelevant to the course. 4. The content of class preparation is irrelevant to what is taught in class. 5. The pass rate of the quiz is lower than 70%.
Overall evaluation result:	100	

To create the ideal class, the school should organize the study of teaching cases, teacher discussions, and open classes and provide teachers with a platform for study, exchange, observation, discussion, and presentation. A strict teaching reflection system should be in place to ask teachers to reflect on a daily basis and organize weekly and monthly reviews. The purpose is to reform the classroom teaching mode, change the teaching mindset and behavior of teachers, limit the lecture within one-third of the class hour, and make sure all students are fully engaged in class.

Classroom teaching is the heart of the whole teaching process. Scientific, regulated, and fine management of daily teaching affairs has far-reaching meaning for improving the benefits of classroom teaching and promoting teachers' growth and the school's sustainable development. In class, the teacher should focus on knowledge that is difficult, easy to neglect, or confusing, and save the trouble for explaining information that students already know, can master on their own, or is too difficult for them to master. The teacher should also do his best to allow students to observe and think by themselves, express their ideas as much as possible, give them the chance to practice, and allow them to draw their own conclusions. The teacher should prepare a teaching plan for each class and try to teach students the scientific way of thinking, carefully design each class and keep the class progress under control, encourage students to follow what's going on in society, apply differentiated teaching to different students in a planned way, give students feedback in a timely manner and improve the teaching effect, give students emotional support, take every assignment seriously, design the homework according to the learning progress of different students, and allow every student to show his or her own individuality.

The school should continue to analyze the teaching quality of each teacher, monitor the teaching process by unit, analyze the teaching quality at the end of every semester, take notes of the findings in a timely manner, and guide teachers to absorb the analysis results and improve themselves accordingly. It should also intensify efforts in teaching survey, track the learning progress of the top students and the underachievers in each class and each grade, develop a personal archive for each of them, and work hard to improve their academic performance.

5. Strengthening leadership and management

A reform leading group shall be formed with the headmaster as the group leader, composed of staff of the teaching affairs department and heads of the teaching research groups for Chinese, mathematics, and English courses. The group shall be responsible for formulating the implementation plan for the school and overseeing its implementation.

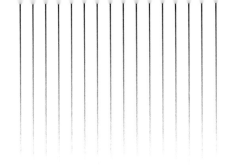

6

The New Education Experiment and Creating the Ideal Classroom

A school is composed of classrooms, and each classroom is itself a miniature school and a standalone community. The quality of a school is heavily shaped by the quality of its classrooms. The ultimate achievements and quality of the New Education Experiment also rest in the story and achievements of each and every classroom. By listing "creating the ideal classroom" as one of its priority actions, the New Education Experiment tries to create a perfect classroom where teachers and students can write life legends together.

I. The New Education Experiment's Idea about Creating the Ideal Classroom

What does creating the ideal classroom mean? Simply speaking, it means to create an individual classroom culture under the guidance of the life narration and moral cultivation theory of the New Education Experiment. To do so,

---

*The above case is contributed by Yu Yuping, a model teacher of the New Education Experiment from Dongzhou Experimental Middle School in Haimen.

teachers and students should draw strength from the child curriculum of the New Education Experiment, "read in the morning and at noon and reflect in the evening," strive to meet the three standards of the ideal class, and make progress together.

In the conventional sense, a school consists of classes and grades. The class is the basic unit of a school and at the bottom of the administrative structure. A class is generally composed of one or a few subject teachers and a group of students, and school education is mainly delivered in the form of class activities. A classroom, or schoolroom, is where teachers give lectures to students, the venue for school education to take place. Therefore, the class is an organizational term while the classroom is a spatial term, but they both bring teachers and students together.

By differentiating these two terms, we want to stress the classroom as a place where teachers and students grow. But it is not just about space, for it witnesses the making of history, the unfolding of stories, and the passage of time. In the words of new education practitioners, it is a place of time.

The reason for the choice of the word "create" is to try to establish association with classroom creators, including not just students, but also teachers whose role is underestimated. Today, people tend to overemphasize the role of students while forgetting that the New Education Experiment is for all people and for all aspects of people's lives. "People" here refers to, without a doubt, students, teachers, parents, and all other stakeholders in the education industry.

"Ideal" represents the vision and the direction of the New Education Experiment. To create the ideal classroom is what we are after, even though we might never be able to reach it. Thus, the idea of creating the ideal classroom is not a harsh criterion, but a mission, a vision. It conveys our value: it is more than a job for us; what we want to do is create something beautiful from our own understanding and pursuit.

In the eyes of new education practitioners, the classroom is always associated with life and for life. It bridges the curriculum and the individual life. A classroom where no life blossoms could never be the ideal one. Life is what the New Education Experiment cherishes the most. A classroom can be ordinary, cold, violent, tyrannical, deceitful, or perfect and heart-warming, and play a completely different role in every individual life spent in it.

According to Japanese educator Manabu Sato, the classroom is the heart of school reform and it is where the educational reform in the real sense is sprouting from. Every classroom has its unique environment and problems. Only through the reform of classroom teaching can we develop new curriculum and create a new learning community.

By creating the ideal classroom, the New Education Experiment hopes to bring home the value of classroom teaching to more teachers and stimulate teachers and students to take actions and work toward the ideal.

II. The Connotation of the Ideal Classroom in the New Education Experiment

Like the school culture, the ideal classroom of the New Education Experiment should have its own mission, vision, and values. It should develop a set of images and symbols, including names, signs, heroes, and models, to differentiate it from the others.

Therefore, the first step to create the ideal classroom is to give it a meaningful name. The name should embody the classroom culture and the collective image of the whole class. Generally speaking, most of the classrooms are named with the numerical system, such as Class 3 of Grade 1 or Class 4 of Grade 2, or teacher Rafe Esquith's Classroom No. 56. This numerical naming method is without doubt the easiest method but also the most boring and mechanical.

In our experimental schools, classroom names often have a special meaning, not cold numbers. Naming a classroom is as important and special as naming a baby. That's why so many headmasters have beaten their brains out to try to come up with a special, beautiful name. In Hainan Middle School in Haimen City, Jiangsu Province, there is a classroom named "Not Ordinary." Headmaster Jiang Bin told us that on their first day at school, the students were amazed by the beautiful campus and the outstanding teachers, sighing, "The campus is really not ordinary!" and "These teachers are really not ordinary!" It was quite a day for them. So at the end of the day, he decided to go for the name "Not Ordinary," to inspire students to be their best and make the class the best in school. This "Not Ordinary" classroom is for not-ordinary students.

There are also many classrooms named after animals or plants such as "Caterpillar" and "Dandelion." They may sound ordinary and simple. But if we can give them special meaning through reading and teaching activities, they will gain life in the heart of students and grow into their common vision. You may give a classroom any name you like, as long as it can really reach the heart of the teachers and students.

The teacher might have spent a lot of time contemplating the right name, or even have come up with a good one, but he must wait for the right moment to propose it. It would be better if the name is proposed after the teacher has spent some time with the students and right after the class has watched some movie or learned a poem on the same theme the name conveys.

The name is just part of the classroom culture, which might also include the emblem, the flag, the anthem, the poem, the motto, the commitment, and so on. The emblem is like the tattoo or the symbol of the class and is generally codeveloped by the entire class by drawing inspiration from the classroom name. The class can hold an emblem-soliciting campaign and work on the winning entries to produce the final version.

In No. 2 Experimental Middle School in Jiaozuo City, Henan Province, there is a classroom named "Bamboo Joint Room." While soliciting the emblem design from the students, the entire class voted for the entry submitted by a student named Liu Haonan. At the bottom of his design are two bamboo joints shooting upward, echoing the name of the classroom. The bamboo leaves at the middle look like sickles, horns, surging sails, and flying wings. At the top of it is a dancing flame, a symbol of the burning, enterprising heart. The emblem might just be a meaningless symbol for outsiders, but for students studying in the "Bamboo Joint Room," it represents their class morale and is co-created by them and their teacher together. For its designer Liu Haonan, the memory of creating the emblem will stay forever in his mind.

The class flag can be used on collective occasions such as sporting events and campus celebrations. It can lighten the atmosphere and build up the class cohesion. It is generally made white cloth or any other color with the emblem design printed on it. The flag can be of various sizes. Small ones can be distributed to students to hold in their hands and big ones can be used for class parades.

The anthem should reflect the vision and morale of the class. It could be an existing song, an original one, or an adapted one. For example, the anthem for the Future Classroom taught by Li Zhenxi is composed by Gu Jianfen, and students in the "Residence by the River and Mountain" in Jiangxian County of Shanxi Province go for the song "I Love You, China" as their class anthem. The lyrics and melody of the anthem should appeal to the taste of students, not adults.

The class poem, like the class anthem, should match with the class vision and name. It can be an original poem written by the students and their teacher or an existing one. For example, the students in "The Little Snail" classroom in Jiangxian County, Shanxi Province, chose the poem "The Little Snail" as their class poem, to motivate students to keep walking, no matter how small the steps are, toward their dream.

The class motto, like the school motto, is a statement of the class's pursuit of value in concise, clear, and thought-provoking language. It can be incorporated as part of the emblem or printed on the flag.

The class commitment is an agreement between teachers and students to create a beautiful future. It often takes the form of oath. For example, in her first letter to parents of her students, teacher Ma Ling wrote, "As a teacher, I promise to make every one of my students a better person." The oath of a student might go like this: "As a student, I believe that I will appreciate the joy of learning and the dignity of life." The teacher and students should take their oath on some major occasion or at some big moment to reinforce the commitment's impact on the mind.

Classroom decoration is also part of the classroom culture. A lack of any meaningful decoration is a sign of cultural poverty. Generally speaking, the classroom setting should appeal to the aesthetic taste of the students. For example, we can keep some potted plants or goldfish in the classroom to bring nature to the children and allow them to see the growth of other lives. The classroom can be painted in a variety of colors. For example, the classroom for low graders can be painted in pink and decorated with the scenes and characters of illustrated books to create a familiar, warm, and safe environment for the children; for senior graders, consider the colors blue, black, or white, and decorations of meaningful paintings and calligraphies to create an intellectual atmosphere; for medium graders, consider the color green and decorations of fresh-looking illustrations of particular oriental style.

Of course, the most important decoration should be created by the teachers and students, such as their photos and written messages. Their artistic works might not be perfect, but should all be posted on the wall because the classroom should be the ideal stage for them to present their works. Therefore, while decorating the classroom, students should consider it as their own magazine, TV station, or archive. It can also be a garden, a display room, to show the potted plants students keep, the ceramic ware they have made, and so on. In summary, the classroom should be co-created by the teachers and students together because it witnesses the journey they will make together. For children, it is vital for them to realize and accept who they are in the classroom.

The classroom culture is also embodied in the unique class calendar. Each classroom should have its own calendar, with a beginning and an ending. The days marked on the calendar are not commercial holidays such as Valentine's Day or April Fool's Day, or traditional Chinese holidays, but important days for the class, such as the birthday of every student, the days of class outings, the start-watching festival, the wheat harvesting festival, the commencement ceremony, and so on. Besides, the last day of each course is also some sort of harvest festival and marked on the calendar to remind the children of the wonderful journey ahead.

Birthday celebrations are a highlight of the New Education Experiment, showing our unique attention to every individual life. It doesn't matter whether there is a birthday cake or not. What matters is to let every child feel that he is being respected and accepted like everyone else, and that his life is dignified and cherished. Among all kinds of celebrations, the birthday story and the birthday poem are the two signature inventions of the experiment. The birthday story should be tailored to the birthday child based on his experience or character and narrated to the whole class on his birthday. The birthday poem could be an original or adapted one, alluding to the name, life experience, or personal traits of the birthday child with special words, just like Charlotte the spider weaving words for Wilbur the pig in *Charlotte's Web*. The biggest day on the calendar should be the day of life celebration. At the end of each semester, the teachers will tell the stories of students and award them, followed by a grand play of life narration. It could be an imaginative fairy-tale play for the first- and second-graders, a thought-provoking and symbolic story for the third- and fourth-graders, and a classic story for the senior graders. On the stage, students speak their mind through the lines and learn from the characters how to make the right choice in dilemma, take one's responsibilities, and live up to one's words.

In the passage of time, some days will become special for some classes. For example, many classes are celebrating the Wanda Festival, which is set up in memory of *The Hundred Dresses* they have read, to remind students not to discriminate against anyone and learn to keep one's words as Maddie does in the book. On that day, teachers and students will look back on the past year and ask themselves, "Has anyone been hurt in the past year in the class? Did I stand up to injustice? Have I drawn my own hundred dresses in the past year?" The Charlotte Festival is also celebrated in many classrooms. It is created to pay tribute to the book *Charlotte's Web* and remind students to become an "important person" in others' lives and weave the net of love. All these ceremonies and celebrations are held to give special meaning to certain days and create heart-warming, special, and long-lasting memories among children.

It should be noted that creating the ideal classroom and developing excellent curriculum are mutually reinforcing. The former is about space while the latter about time. Only a classroom with an excellent new education curriculum is the ideal one. Without an excellent curriculum, students won't be able to blossom in the classroom. Only when the new education curriculum matures can the New Education Experiment truly take root; only when the complete new education curriculum system takes form can the new education edifice take form. Therefore, the curriculum is key to the future of our new education dream.

Then what is the key to the creation of the ideal classroom? I think the ideal classroom should have the following three traits.

First, it should pool all the beautiful things. It should be a place where the vision, the culture, and the curriculum of new education meet and perfectly blend into each other. It is where teachers bring the best knowledge of their respective subject and the most useful things for the rest of the students' lives to the students. Likewise, a school should be where all the great things meet, to introduce students to the most wonderful treasure of the mankind, and help students discover who they are and realize their full potential.

Second, it should cherish every individual life. The ideal classroom allows life to blossom and would never neglect any of the children. No individual in the classroom should be forgotten. Instead, every life in it deserves special attention and support. Why do we go through all the trouble to read poems on birthdays, to stage the life narration play, or present life awards? It is because we cherish every life. The life narration play, unlike any other school play, involves all the students in the class, and the life award, unlike other school awards, is for every student and specially named after the characters, animals, and stories of the books students have read in the past semester. There are some potted plants and pet animals in the ideal classroom to show students growth and strength. In the ideal classroom, every life is cherished and no one is neglected. The New Education Experiment makes a special point of paying more attention and offering more support to the vulnerable and the disadvantaged to increase the possibilities of their lives.

Third, every day counts in the ideal classroom. In the ideal classroom, every day should be well spent and become special and memorable for the teachers and students. To mark the days, special celebrations and festivals are staged in the ideal classroom. Here, every day is special and important, worth looking forward to. The ideal classroom should be a place where students long to be, a stage where teachers and students make progress together. Teachers should make sure that students make the most of every day in the ideal classroom. At the end of each day, you should ask yourself: How is the day going? Have the children learned something? Am I a better person than yesterday? If all your answers are yes, and if every day spent in the classroom is memorable for the children, then congratulations—you have created the ideal classroom.

III. Creating the Ideal Classroom: Case Study
Teacher Yu Yuping's Lily Class in Haimen

Every year, I will read to my new students the following story about the lily flower:

> A lily seed is blown away mercilessly to a distant cliff, greeted with nothing but the hostility of weeds and the sarcasm of bees and butterflies. But the lily seed says to herself: I will blossom for I know I have beautiful flowers, this is my mission and I want to prove the value of my existence. Therefore she takes in moisture and enjoys the sunlight as much as she can. She stretches her root deep downward … eventually one day she greets the world with snow-white flowers and let the wind carry all her seeds to every corner of the valley.

Then I will ask the attentive children: Which is happy and beautiful, the lily or the weeds? All the children would vote for the lily flower; they all want to be like the lily, to find a dream of their own, to work hard for it, see it blossom and make the world a better place. It is my firm belief that every child is like a lily, with the innate eagerness to blossom.

I often stayed up late on the night before the first day of every school year, writing greeting messages to every single student of the class—the name list wouldn't reach me until three or four o'clock in the afternoon.

Normally on the first day at school, the name badge prepared by the school won't be ready. So how could I help the students break the ice and get to know each other quickly? I came up with the idea to design name cards for them. The front of the name card reads "I will blossom for I know I have beautiful flowers," a sentence printed in red at the top. At the center of it are three light-blue stars where students will write their name down. At the bottom are a few white lily flowers. The back of the name card carries the greeting message I wrote for each of the students.

For example, my message for Shuming is: A good book will lead you to a wonderful world and a cup of tea will give you the taste of tranquil life. Quiet and thoughtful as you are, I'm sure you will become a great mind like Ji Xianlin after you grow up.

My message for Shuaihan: I guess you are a bookish boy, graceful in manners, witty in language, and gentle in character.

My message for Shiheng: You must be a girl with eternal childlike innocence and poetic beauty as your name suggests. You look pure and smart and I believe you will leave eternal goodness behind.

My message for Yingran: I like your crystal heart, your devotion to study, and your love of reading. I believe some day you will be a shining star of the 0924 Class.

My message for Haoyu: I guess you are an ambitious, optimistic, and broad-hearted girl, aren't you? I really like such girls. Let's create a beautiful future together.

One by one, the name cards carry my best wishes and goodwill to each of the students.

Before the students arrived, I cleaned the classroom thoroughly, put the textbook neatly on the right corner of each desk, pasted the student number on the right corner, and placed the student name card right at the middle of each desk. On the front blackboard I wrote: "You Make 0924 a Better Place," and drew lily flowers as the background pattern. Below it I wrote down the name of subject teachers. On the back blackboard I copied the lyrics of "The Loving Family." The shelves were stacked with books accumulated by graduates and me. I did all this to give the new students an impression that this was a warm, book-loving class and to win their respect for it.

On the first day of the school year, I asked a student to greet the other new students at the door, saying with a smile: "Hello, please follow me. I will take you to your seat." Then the greeted student would take his place to welcome and take the next newcomer to his seat. In this way, every student has the chance to act as the host of the class.

After all the students took their seat, the first class began. I asked them to read their name card, the back side first, then the front side. I saw smiles rise on their faces. Then I asked them to read the sentence on the front and tell me what it meant and what the three stars were for. The class answered in one voice, "They are for us to write our names." When I asked them why write your name on the stars, they gave me the most amazing answers: "It's because you hope we will shine like the stars some day" and "It's because you hope we will stay together, united like the stars. There are three of them because you want us to know that one sparrow doesn't make spring and it's better to shine with others than shine alone."

Then I invited the students to come forward one by one to explain the meaning of their name, which they did with ease and confidence. Each name conveys the best wishes of the parents.

Then I read them the essay "The Lily Flower in the Heartland" written by Lin Qingxuan, an essayist from Taiwan, and asked them to name the class. So that's how my Lily Class was born.

I asked the students to repeat the following: "I will blossom for I know I have beautiful flowers. This is my mission and I want to prove the value of my existence."

I wanted them to appreciate what the lily flower represented and cast the lily seed in their heart, the desire to blossom into a beautiful lily in this new environment.

Now, on every morning, students of the Lily Class will naturally go to the flowerbeds, either from the dormitory or home, take out their book, and start reading.

They are completely absorbed in the book they are holding, regardless of the walking steps, talking voices, distant calls, and traffic horns on the road. This is the most beautiful scene in the morning.

But the students didn't appreciate the beauty of reading at first.

At first, while they were reading by the flowerbed, some students couldn't help but turn their head up to see who was coming in or out, or listen to the chirping of birds. Sometimes some passing ants on the ground would distract them for a while.

I never criticize or say anything harsh for such behavior. One day, I showed them the photos I took of them reading in the morning, under the theme "The Beauty of Focus."

There was no more mind-drifting at the flowerbed the next morning. The children started to resist the distractions in the surroundings and concentrate on the book consciously.

But after a while, I noticed another problem. Sometimes, even when the students kept their eyes on the book, their mind was not processing. I think this happened in class, too.

So I took many close photos of the students' eyes. I showed them the photos and asked them to categorize. The students were sharp enough to divide the eyes I captured into "intellectual eyes," "confusing eyes," and "lost eyes." I asked them which were more beautiful in the eyes of bystanders. Students captured with "confusing eyes" and "lost eyes" gave the answer by lowering their head out of shame.

Then I asked those students captured with "intellectual eyes" how they managed to concentrate. Many of them mentioned that they would set goals and tasks before they started reading and then what they needed to do was concentrate on accomplishing them one by one. "How did that make you feel?" "Peaceful and fulfilled."

These "intellectual" children became the envy of those "confused" and "lost" children.

From then on, there was no more mind-empty reading at the flowerbed.

Every morning, every noon, and every evening, among the people lining up at the dining hall, you can see two lines of students waiting while holding a book in their hands. They are absorbed in the books despite the laughter, walking steps, and the smell of freshly cooked dishes.

Reading is the best pacifier for the mind in moments of anxiety.

I once asked the students to observe the behavior of people lining up in the chaotic, hustling dining hall and guess what was in their mind.

Back in the classroom, the children started to compare notes.

"Most of the people stood on their tiptoes to count the number of people lined up before them. One kid even counted three times. His eyebrows furrowed and his eyes were anxious."

"He was starving and couldn't wait to eat."

"Some students were making fun of each other, but they looked bored. It's as if they were doing that to kill the time."

"It's because they were bored, felt empty, but had to stay there."

"Some were waiting for their turn patiently, but it seemed dull and boring."

Then I asked, "It seems that idleness doesn't make one look good, but is a kind of mental torture. Can we make a change?"

Some students suggested bringing a book to the dining hall for reading would keep you from making loud noises, looking around or anxious, or wasting your time in line.

I said, "We should all mind our manners in the dining hall so that one day there will be no loud noises there. I hope one day we will see no one idling their time away, but only readers making the most of their free time in public spaces."

The student to give the first class lecture was Jiang Yuyang. That day, she came to the lecture hall early to prepare for the lecture. Then two classes of students arrived, 92 of them in total, and filled the lecture hall. There was no extra seat for me, so I had to stand against the southern wall.

After the light was off, "lecturer" Yuyang started to play her PowerPoint slides on the screen.

All the other students had their eyes fixed on the screen, full of curiosity, envy, and eagerness.

The lecture began: "My presentation today is about preparation, in-class study, and review."

"In class, we should keep our chin and chest up, and stay fresh." Hearing that, the audience suddenly straightened their back, and their heads sprung up as fresh as spring bamboos.

Then the light was turned back on. Yuyang stood up and went to the blackboard. She drew a notebook on it with chalk, attracting the audience's eyes away from the screen to the blackboard.

She demonstrated and explained the way she took notes and was asked some questions. Then after discussing with the audience, she came up with a better way to take notes.

After the lecture, I asked the audience to recall what they had just learned.

That was our first lecture by students and for students. It worked surprisingly well.

I asked Yuyang the "lecturer": "How much time have you spent reading the book and preparing the presentation?"

She said with a smile, "I have read the book twice to choose the most useful learning methods for us for today's presentation. I worked on the slides last night until one or two o'clock in the early morning."

"Are you tired?"

"A little bit. But I felt so good standing here and explaining myself to the attentive audience, and I'm glad they find my presentation very useful. Besides, after the presentation, I feel like these methods I introduced are really mine, even though I didn't invent them in the first place."

I laughed, "Let me summarize it for you: the happiest person is a person useful for the others. The more value you have for others, the happier you are."

Then I asked the audience, "What do you think of the lecture? Do you want to have a try?"

The audience said the lecture revealed their weakness in learning and introduced them to some good learning methods. They found it really helpful and hoped they could also have the chance to introduce some good books to the class.

"Then let's have one lecture by one or more students each week to recommend one book to the rest of the class," I said as I jumped on the opportunity.

There are no dormitory buildings on the new campus, so we have to take the school bus to the new campus every morning and back to the old campus every evening. The ride takes about ten minutes.

I asked the students to say hello to the driver every time they get on the bus. So every morning when they are all onboard, the students would say good morning to the driver in one voice and then say goodbye before they get off. But as time passed, I could tell some students didn't mean what they said.

Therefore, one day, I held a class meeting on the theme of "Hello." I asked the students what "hello" meant. Some said it was equivalent to "I hope everything goes well with you," and some said it was equivalent to "I wish you all the best." I said, "Generally speaking, saying hello to others is not a tradition in China. But it conveys our sincere and good wishes for others. One that delivers sincere, good wishes to others is rich in goodness and the one that receives such good wishes is made happy by the kindness shown to him." I continued, "Have you noticed the facial expression of the driver when you say hello to him every day?" Some students replied, "He smiled." I said, "Yes. He smiled because he was touched by your kindness and warmth. When the driver is happy, the ride will be safe. He must have thought to himself: these children are so adorable and I should make sure they get to school safe and sound. This is how your kindness to the driver will be paid back. A harmonious interpersonal relationship did make our short trip more enjoyable, didn't it?"

Another question followed, "What if there was no driver for us?"

The children were smart enough to realize that "We would have less time for study. We owe that to the driver."

"You bet. From now on, you should really mean it when you say hello or thank you to the driver. Another quick question: who else should we say hello and thank you to?"

"The teachers. Without them, we would still be uncivilized human beings."

"The workers in the dining hall. Without them, we would starve."

"The cleaning ladies in the restrooms. Without them, the restrooms would be too dirty to use."

"Everyone, because we couldn't live without the work of everyone else."

I concluded, "Good. Since you all know that we cannot live without others, from now on, let's learn to say hello to all the rest of the people."

From that day on, students' greetings were no longer limited to the school bus. At the dining hall, they would say thank you to the worker behind the counter for delivering the food and receive a smile in return. This small change has made the dining hall more loving and more heartwarming.

With absolute trust in children's aspiration for growth, I will ask them to write their monthly and semester goals and then keep motivating them toward the goals. When they have setbacks and feel frustrated, I will tell them the story about the petrel and the sparrow: though the sparrow flies higher, it is the persistent petrel that eventually crosses the sea. I would also show them the movie *Kungfu Panda*, to boost their confidence in their potential. I would sing with them the song "The Little Snail": "Step by step, I will keep going upward. My dream is too big to be confined. One day, I will have a sky of my own." I would also listen to the music "The Symphony of Fate" with them and shout with them: "I will seize fate by its throat!" I would do all I can to make them believe that all the bad times will pass and there is no need to cry over spilled milk.

Motivation is the keyword of all my educational activities. I would tell students stories of inspirational role models: graduates who are working at the embassy, have translated for the secretary general of the Olympic Games Organizing Committee, and are studying for a doctoral degree in the United States with a scholarship. All I want to stress is that these role models are not super brains or geniuses, but they know what they want and stick to it. I would ask the students to read biographies of some great names and tell them these people are known for their tremendous contribution to the world and their dedication to their dream.

During holidays and summer/winter vacations, I would fly to Singapore or the United Kingdom with the students. After taking part in the training program of Singapore Dunman High School, some students have decided to study in Singapore after graduation and are working harder toward the goal. The visit to the United Kingdom, especially Cambridge University, was so impressive that one of the ninth-grade students managed to pass the TOEFL exam in just two months—the exam is even challenging for college students. In the last two months of the ninth grade, a girl whose academic performance was dragged down by her illness worked hard day and night, with the encouragement of her teacher, and was eventually admitted into her dream school—Haimen High School.

You should have faith that every child is born to blossom like the lily seed and learning is in the students' nature. We should never judge the future of a child based on his IQ. Teachers and parents have the duty to guide children to a good, upbeat life, protect their innocence, and enable them to shine.

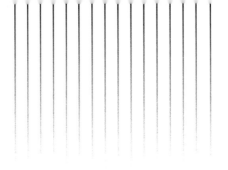

7

The New Education Experiment and Developing Excellent Curriculum

I.   The New Education Outlook on Curriculum
II. The Excellent Curriculum Structure of New Education
III. Case Study*

The New Education Experiment attaches great importance to curriculum. The diversity and quality of curriculum will decide the richness and quality of students' lives. By developing excellent curriculum, we mean to encourage teachers' secondary development, integration, and innovation of textbooks while following the national, local, and school-specific curriculum, in order to create a "happy and all-around educational life" and turn the classroom into the gathering hub of greatness and goodness. While implementing the curriculum, teachers shall lead students through collaborative and exploratory study; establish connection between book knowledge, the outside world, and their inner self; translate the knowledge they have learned into wisdom; and enrich the life of both teachers and students.

For a dozen years, the new education community has developed a set of excellent curriculum and made useful explorations in theory and practice.

---

*The above case is contributed by Song Xinju, a model teacher of the New Education Experiment in Jiaozuo City, Henan Province.

I. The New Education Outlook on Curriculum

Curriculum is generally considered the sum of educational contents chosen to realize the goals of school education. As far as the research and development process is concerned, there are four kinds of courses: subject courses, activity courses, general courses, and implicit courses. Subject courses are traditionally further divided into instrumental subjects (Chinese, mathematics, and foreign language), social sciences subjects (moral education, politics, history, geography, etc.), natural sciences subjects (nature, biology, physics, and chemistry), and skills subjects (physical education, music, fine arts, labor skills, vocational guidance, etc.). Activity courses generally include hands-on operation, artistic and literary creation, entertainment and performances, survey and research, and exchange and discussion. General courses are generally interdisciplinary, including knowledge-standard courses and social-standard courses. Implicit courses are relative to all the above explicit courses, unofficial, unintended experience students gain in the school environment but unspecified in the school policy or teaching plan. Such courses are uncertain, compulsory, and sustainable. According to statistical data, subject courses take up nearly 80 percent of class hours, among which instrumental subjects comprise over 50 percent, in schools providing compulsory education.

The New Education Experiment holds that curriculum and teaching are closely interrelated and mutually reinforcing, inseparable from each other. Without teaching, curriculum is only a pile of cold files; without curriculum, teaching is like a building without a foundation. In other words, to teach students how to fish, both the teaching activity and the curriculum are needed.

If we compare the curriculum to a people-centered journey with a starting point and a destination, then the so-called excellent curriculum is the journey that brings you to the established goals and makes you feel complete and happy along the way. The excellent curriculum represents the direction of our pursuit, our commitment to the future. It is the mission and responsibility of us new education practitioners to create excellent curriculum for students.

The excellent curriculum should have the following features. First, it should be able to "create a happy, all-around educational life for teachers and students." By "happy" we mean that the learning process should be enjoyable and exciting, able to raise students' expectations for the future, and should not be at the expense of the current happy life of students. By "complete" we mean that the school should insist on the harmonious mental and physical development of students; promote values of truth, goodness, and beauty; gather goodness and greatness; and create more possibilities for students. In other words, the excellent curriculum should serve the ultimate purpose of individual happiness and completeness.

Second, it should respect the physical and mental development pattern of students and proceed from students' development. It should reflect the physical and mental development characteristics of students in each stage as much as possible, develop their zone of proximal development to the utmost, and meet their needs for development.

Third, the excellent curriculum should respect the romantic feelings of learners, including their initial perceptions of life: confusion, curiosity, fascination with beauty, and so on. Such feelings are of special meaning in the initial stage of learning. Without them, the learner will find it hard to keep going. Enforcing discipline on learners will destroy the beauty of learning and the romantic impulse for precision learning. Through precision learning, or detailed analysis of facts, the learner will be able to form a specific, systematic idea of knowledge learned. After that, the learner should be able to be freed from rigid, specific rules, stop fretting about detailed knowledge, actively employ principles, and take the initiative to apply what he has learned. The excellent curriculum should be all-embracing, with focal precision. There is no way and no need to learn all the knowledge, but we do need to dive deep into certain subjects. Therefore, a hallmark of the excellent curriculum is to help students accumulate expert knowledge in certain areas within limited time.

Fourth, the excellent curriculum should be able to reach the heart of learners and be relevant to their life. It should not be a mere sum of dead knowledge, but should be able to impact the heart, the mind, and the soul.

Fifth, the excellent curriculum should arouse deep empathy between knowledge and life. As far as contents are concerned, the excellent curriculum stresses the importance of incorporating knowledge and experience into the students' lives. It asks teachers to teach based on scenarios and to learn from students. Eventually, the lives of both teachers and students will be enriched and stimulated through the implementation of the excellent curriculum.

II. The Excellent Curriculum Structure of New Education

Based on the life course, the excellent curriculum of new education features citizen courses (goodness), artistic courses (beauty), and intellectual courses (truth), supplemented with specialty courses (individuality).

The life course is officially named the "New Life Education." It is a general course aimed to guide students to understand and appreciate the value of life, respect life, and turn the possibilities of life into reality. Upholding the principle of "creating a happy, all-around educational life," it proceeds from the idea of life, including man's natural life, social life, and spiritual life; teaches knowledge on safety, health, social intercourse, cultivation, values, faiths, and so on; and tries to guide students to cherish life, make the best of their life, and live a happy, fulfilled life.

The New Education Experiment has long attached importance to life education. In 2004, we proposed six actions (new parent education, new citizen education, new life education, new vocational education, new teacher education, and new rural education), included "new life education" into our research scope, and put forth the five dimensions and three goals for it. In the same year, we co-organized with the Soong Ching Ling Foundation China's first advanced workshop for teachers on life education for teenagers. Members of our research group, Yuan Weixing, Xu Xinhai, and Chen Guo'an, have coedited textbooks and readings such as *The Lesson on Life*, *Life Education*, *Life and Safety*, and *The 18 Class Meetings*. In 2015, we combed through the theories and practices on life education and developed the curriculum and textbooks on new life education targeting kindergarten to high schools under the title "For Longer, More Expansive and Deeper Life," which has been in trial use in our experimental schools since 2016.

If the life course addresses issues about individual health and wellness, then citizen courses are about the rights, responsibilities, and obligations of a social person. They are designed to cultivate modern citizens who respect social ethics; identify with, understand, obey, and safeguard the Constitution; follow and take part in public affairs; think independently; do not shy from responsibilities; and identify with traditional national culture. They cover the ethics, values, citizenship knowledge, and participatory skills of modern citizens. Specifically, ethics refer to virtues such as benevolence, forgiveness, gratitude, friendship, rituals, honesty, responsibility, dignity, cooperation, and so on. Values include freedom, equality, human rights, democracy, rule of law, justice, peace, patriotism, pursuit of truth, and harmonious coexistence with nature. Citizenship knowledge covers knowledge about state and government, democratic politics, the political party system, judicial justice, social public life, and rights and responsibilities of citizens. Participatory skills refer to a citizen's basic abilities to part take in public life, such as the abilities of communication, speech, discussion, organization, participating in elections, handling disputes, protecting one's interests, and filing complaints or making suggestions to the responsible department or the press.

Citizenship education should be included into not just evening reflection sessions, class meetings, the books read, fairy-tale plays staged, and movies watched, but also class ceremonies, birthday celebrations, and end-of-semester celebrations. We have made some useful attempts in this regard. In 2005, we held the annual meeting themed on "New Moral Education, New Citizens" in Chengdu and edited and published the eight-volume textbook *Readings for New Citizens*, targeting students from primary school to high school. This textbook series is known as "the first complete set of citizenship readings targeting students from primary school to high school since the founding of the People's Republic of China in 1949."

Artistic education is important in the excellent curriculum of new education. The New Education Experiment holds that for individuals, artistic education will give them a strong impetus for early development and offer them a path for improving qualities and capabilities. For schools, artistic education binds other fragmented subjects like adhesive and stimulates students when they are tired. For families, it adds poetic elements into daily life and makes moral education enjoyable. For the society, it unites different social groups and enhances social cohesion and innovation capacity. For the nation, it carries forward the spirit and culture of the nation. For the mankind, it gives us another perspective of looking at the world and opens another door to the world.

The artistic education promoted by the New Education Experiment is to allow students, while learning about arts, appreciating outstanding artworks, and mastering skills for artistic creation, to develop the mindset, taste, and spirit of artists; inherit outstanding human culture; enrich the spiritual world; and better cultivate their personality.

The purpose is not to turn students into professional artists, or to spot and cultivate artistic talents, but to set students' nature free, and help them develop eyes and tastes for arts. It is from arts (the nature of students), through arts (as a prevalent intermediary agent), and for arts (to live an artistic life). It aims to allow students a happy and complete life.

The New Education Experiment has launched many general art courses of distinct characteristics such as the course on listening, reading, drawing, and speech; the life narration course; the drama course; and the movie course, breaking the boundaries between arts and other subjects and exploring a new way for non-arts teachers to engage in artistic education.

Intellectual courses, similar to courses on natural and social sciences we are familiar with, include Chinese, mathematics, foreign language, science (or physics, chemistry, or biology), history, and society (or history and geography), which make up the chunk of the excellent curriculum. The name reflects our thoughts on the nature of these courses. Such courses are not to simply pass down knowledge, but to foster wisdom to master knowledge in various fields and abilities to apply knowledge. Knowledge is the medium in this process. We then turn knowledge into intellect and wisdom.

The implementation of intellectual courses must follow some special rules. Intellectual cultivation is different from moral cultivation (citizen courses) and spiritual cultivation (artistic courses). Many schools used to implement most courses stipulated by the state by means of lecture and exam, and as a result turn moral, artistic, and physical education into part of intellectual education. Knowledge learned in this way is dead and won't be incorporated into students' real life. It doesn't go with the basic educational law to assess the citizen courses, moral courses, and artistic courses including fine arts courses and music courses via written exams.

Intellectual courses of new education have two missions. First, they should be developed based on the national curriculum and meet the three standards of the ideal class with the given content. Second, in addition to stipulated content, they should include extracurricular knowledge, which is referred to as the second syllabus by Suhomlinski, personal understanding of the subject in question, and knowledge one deems necessary. "Living by the Lunar Calendar" is one such course.

The above life course, citizen courses, artistic courses, and intellectual courses have basically covered all that is needed for "creating a happy, all-around educational life" and "becoming a happy, complete, and free person." As the basis, life education should run through the whole educational process, but kindergartens, primary schools, and middle schools may have their respective priorities and carry out education on goodness (via citizen courses), beauty (artistic courses), and truth (intellectual courses) according to the character-istics of students' physical and mental development. In addition, the New Edu-cation Experiment has proposed courses for developing the individuality of students and the specialty of schools.

From the above rough description of the new education curriculum structure, we can see that there is a great ambition behind it. But while designing courses, we uphold the principle "less is more" and stay vigilant over leap-forward in educational reform. We also find our hands tight as a non-governmental orga-nization. What we have done is only a tiny part of our blueprint. We will keep working to turn the vision into reality step by step. But in another sense, there might not be a definite end to this journey because the world is ever-changing, students come and go, and the curriculum needs to be updated accordingly. The process will never end. But the excellent curriculum structure will act as a guiding map to take us closer to our dream step by step.

III. Case Study

Developing excellent curriculum is the unshakable duty of the New Education Experiment because it must have its own complete curriculum system for the sake of sustainable development. Though still far away from our dream, we have launched projects such as morning reading, One Thing per Month, and fairy-tale plays in recent years, and have developed courses such as "Living with the Lunar Calendar," which are widely adopted and warmly welcomed in schools nationwide. Our experimental zones and schools have made fruitful attempts on their own, such as the Top Ten Virtues course developed by Yinhe Experimental Primary School in Xiaoshan and the School Ceremony course launched in Jiangxian County. The popularity of the Experiment is partly attributed to these ever-improving and adapting courses.

i. Preparation

It is September and the summer heat is still lingering, reluctant to go away. Every student will bring a bottle of water to the school every day. One day, it suddenly dawned on a student to shake the bottle and turn it upside down. And there appeared a whirlpool! He shared this exciting discovery with me and with his classmates. This chance discovery aroused the students' interest in science.

By opening the science course, we hope to teach some basic science of everyday life to the students so that they can apply it to their real life and gradually foster good habits and lifestyles, understand the process and methods of scientific research, try research projects, gradually learn to analyze and think in the scientific way, stay curious about their surroundings, and be able to think big and out of the box while respecting scientific evidence.

Based on the mental and physical development characteristics of the students, we designed some mini-topics for the science course. One of them is dinosaurs. The preparation for the dinosaur week takes the following steps:

1. Deliberating on the standards of the science course for low- and medium-graders based on children's physical and mental development characteristics, recommending courses with ascending degree of difficulty, and eventually forming a course system.
2. Collecting materials on dinosaurs, such as dinosaur documentaries presented by CCTV-10 or other channels of CCTV, the popular science reading *The Magic School Bus: In the Time of the Dinosaurs*, guidebooks on dinosaur drawing, paper-folding and clay-sculpting, as well as the making of dinosaur posters, and so on.
3. Choosing popular science readings on dinosaurs to increase students' knowledge about the topic, such as *The Magic School Bus: In the Time of the Dinosaurs*, *What Is What: Dinosaurs*, *a Look Back on the Discovery of Dinosaurs*, and *The Times of Dinosaurs*.
4. Dividing labor with the parent committee and engaging parents in the design and implementation of the course.

ii. Implementation

The one-week science course on dinosaurs consists of a launch ceremony, colorful learning activities, and a closing ceremony.

Specifically through the learning activities, students will learn the types of dinosaurs, the reason for their extinction, dinosaur drawing, paper-folding and clay-sculpting, and the excavation of dinosaur fossils, and stage a charity sale of DIY dinosaur products.

The course also includes a launch ceremony and a closing ceremony. Core monies are important in the new education curriculum structure because they make ordinary days special and create special memories for students.

a. The Launch

Before the course kicked off, the teacher sent a text message to parents of the class: "Dear parents, we are about to launch a one-week comprehensive course on dinosaurs. We will read *The Magic School Bus: In the Time of the Dinosaurs* to learn about the world where dinosaurs lived, their types, and the reason for their extinction. We will read heartwarming stories about dinosaurs, learn about the excavation of dinosaur fossils, DIY dinosaur products, and stage a charity sale of them. We have so many things to do in the following week. I really appreciate your help, encouragement, and support." Within half an hour, the teacher received a lot of replies from the parents. They showed full understanding and support via text message, phone call, and QQ. Some volunteered immediately: "I can teach the kids how to draw dinosaurs." "I have just learned paper-folding from the Internet. I can teach children how to do the dinosaur paper-folding." "I know there are molded dinosaur fossils for teaching purposes for sale on the Internet. They can be very useful for the science course." "I don't have deft hands, but I can contribute to classroom setting."

The morale was high. With the generous support of parents, the teacher was confident to deliver all the contents of the course. The mother of a student named Yang Zishang offered to buy molded dinosaur fossils from the Internet as a surprise gift for the children at the opening ceremony.

So the science course started.

The theme of the launch ceremony was "Into the Dinosaur World, Unraveling the Mystery of Science." And its mission was to prepare the students for what to do in the following week.

First, the teacher showed a video about dinosaurs, bringing children back to the long-gone world.

Then pictures of dinosaurs of different types, living in different ages were shown to arouse children's strong interest. They were followed by the heartwarming story *I Am a Tyrannosaurus*, written by Tatsuya Miyanishi. Then the students were told what to prepare for the one-week courses and given the molded dinosaur fossils. The children were excited and couldn't wait to start the dinosaur week.

b. Colorful Learning Activities

Science education should proceed from mankind's inner curiosity about mysteries of the natural world. It is in our DNA. Dinosaurs were once the biggest animals on Earth and have long been an object of interest for children. The most important job of teachers and parents is to help children unravel the mystery of science, design the process to do so, and develop the skills necessary for scientific research from the experience.

The dinosaur week was kicked off.

On the first day, the students were asked to bring their own dinosaur toys to the classroom and exchange with classmates. Toy exchanging and playing aroused children's great interest in and curiosity about the dinosaur world and filled them with great excitement for the upcoming science course.

The Magic School Bus: In the Time of the Dinosaurs was chosen as the main textbook for the week. It takes the students into the remote and mysterious land of dinosaurs, shows them their living environment, types, and the reasons for their extinction.

Documentaries about dinosaurs were screened during major class intervals on a daily basis, including the *Animal World: Dinosaurs Return to Life* produced by CCTV and *Into Science—Reasons for the Extinction of Dinosaurs* produced by CCTV-10. They entertained the children with valuable popular science knowledge during breaks that would otherwise have been wasted on chasing around.

In addition, a heartwarming dinosaur story created by Tatsuya Miyanishi was shared every day, including *I Am a Tyrannosaurus, You Are My Best Friend, You Look Yummy!*, and *I Will Love You Forever*.

In the morning, the students would learn theme-specific popular science information about dinosaurs. In the afternoon, they would engage in thematic hands-on activities, such as drawing dinosaurs, narrating the characteristics of dinosaurs, paper-folding dinosaurs, clay-sculpting dinosaurs, excavating molded dinosaur fossils, and selling DIY dinosaur products for charity.

The drawing class was run by the mother of Xie Yuchen. She first analyzed the characteristics of each type of dinosaur and the geographical environment where they lived before teaching the students to draw. She asked the class to create the living environment, including plants, for dinosaurs with their imagination. A special area in the classroom was reserved for the students to display their finished drawings. Each child had the opportunity to show their drawing and share with the rest of the class their favorite dinosaur, its physical features, what it ate, how it lived, and so on. In this way, students gradually and unconsciously had a better and more precise picture of the features of different types of dinosaurs and their living environment. What a fun way to learn science!

The mother of Wang Yao taught the students how to fold paper dinosaurs, including the Brachiosaurus and the Diplodocus, by explaining the paper-folding techniques and the physical features of the dinosaurs. The students once again proved their deftness. Huang Feixiang insisted on making a set of three paper dinosaurs: the child dinosaur with its dad and mom—a complete family. Wang Yao's mother shared her experience on QQ Zone: "I gave a paper-folding class to my daughter and her classmates. The students were excited and attentive in class. The paper dinosaurs came out in different shapes from their deft hands. Everyone enjoyed the process. It is all we have worked for."

The mother of Song Yunshu showed the students how to sculpt dinosaurs with clay dug out from the farmland in her hometown near the Yellow River. In the tiny hands of students, the soft clay was soon turned into small dinosaurs of various shapes.

All the students were particularly excited about the day when they would have the chance to try excavating molded dinosaur fossils. First, with the help of *Small Newton the Science Museum*, they learned the formation of dinosaur fossils in detail, then watched a 3-D animation video about the formation, discovery, excavation, transportation, repair, and molding of fossils. The students were awed by the dedication of scientists and the fearlessness of archeologists at field work as shown in the video.

With molded fossils passed down and desks covered with newspapers, the simulated excavation experience began. The classroom suddenly went silent; you could only hear the breath of the students. When the "fossil" was brought to light by their hands, the students were beaming. Their hands were painted white by the lime, which their mind was too absorbed to notice. Without a doubt, the students had learned how to concentrate on what they were doing until it was done.

Indeed, the dinosaur week included a great variety of contents delivered in a variety of forms and gave students many opportunities to practice and think. Persistence, expression of inner feelings, creative thinking, and all the other qualities the students had shown in the process, aren't they the must-cultivate qualities for life? Against this standard, the course is indeed impressive for its abundant contents, effectiveness, connotation, and denotation, as well as the thoughts and changes it triggered. It has really changed our mindset and illuminated our future with the power of science.

We vowed to take the children into the dinosaur world. For this purpose, we made particular efforts to create the dinosaur culture and immerse the students in it.

Classroom setting was a must. On Wednesday, the mother of Wang Yuetong, the mother of Huang Feixiang, and the mother of Wang Yao spent the afternoon threading all the paper dinosaurs folded by the students in an illustrated book store and waited until the class was over to hang them in the classroom. "Dinosaurs" were everywhere from ceiling to floor, from the front door to the back door, from the front blackboard to the back blackboard, and on all the four walls of the classroom, turning the classroom into a land of dinosaurs. Immersion learning is what the child curriculum has been advocating.

c. The Closing

When the exciting dinosaur week approached an end, I started to think about its closing ceremony. I planned a big one, which was not to be staged in the classroom as before, but in the Longquan Lake Park, the biggest park of the local community.

The first step was to design posters, including e-posters and paper posters. Poster design was considered a bonus of the course. The Mother of Song Yunshu offered to teach the students how to design and make posters, including the theme, illustrations, the color combination, and the fonts of posters, and the writing of the producer and the date of production. Soon the students started to put their life vitality into the posters.

What to do with the finished posters? I took a few students with their posters to the headmaster's office and consulted the headmaster where to put up the posters. Then the students visited other classes one by one in every grade to introduce the dinosaur week program and put up the poster for the closing ceremony.

Meanwhile, the parent committee divided the labor. The mother of Feixiang was responsible for choosing the venue for the closing ceremony, the mother of Wang Yao for logistics, the mother of Yuetong and that of Jujing for maintaining a good order at the venue site, and Yunshu's mother for providing on-site technical support.

The closing ceremony consisted of five parts: storytelling by Cui Zhengx-uan's mother, drawing dinosaurs with colored pencils, speeches on dinosaurs, dinosaur clay-sculpting, and the charity sale.

Cui's mother chose a little-known illustrated book on dinosaurs from the Moguli Illustrated Book Store to share with the students. When the story began, the children gathered quietly around Cui's mother, with their eyes fixed on the storyteller and minds absorbed in the remote world of dinosaurs. To lighten the atmosphere, Cui's mother shot interesting questions such as "Which was the biggest and the smallest dinosaur?" "Which was the first dinosaur on Earth?" "Which was the last dinosaur on Earth?" "Which dinosaur had the longest teeth?" "Which dinosaur was the first to be found with feathers?" The students rushed to answer with big smiles on their faces, bringing the story-telling session to its climax.

It was then time to draw dinosaurs. The students took out their drawing pencils and started to work in groups of three and four. Then they were divided into groups, with eight students each, to share with the rest of the class the name and features of the dinosaur on their drawing. In the paper-folding session, the students had already mastered the folding techniques. Their hands moved deftly while they told each other which dinosaur they were folding. The climax of the day arrived with the sculpting session. Some students even brought porcelain pans and other ware to the class. The dinosaur sculptures they made were so vivid. "This is the Triceratops." "This one is called Quetzalcoatlus." "This one in my hand is a Tyrannosaurus." "Mom, don't touch it. The clay is a little dry now.

I need to spray some water on it first." Though their hands were dirty with clay, the students were all beaming at the sight of the sculpture they created.

"Will it sell? Will anyone want to buy it?" The students were excited about the charity sale. "Auntie, this is called Triceratops. It's pretty. Buy it and you'll get one more DIY for free." "Uncle, please come and take a look." The parents were worried about the sale, afraid that the children's enthusiasm would be dampened if their sculptures couldn't sell. But the children were optimistic and confident. The price didn't matter, as long as it could sell. One yuan was OK, and even five jiao was acceptable. The sale went on much better than imagined. Wang Yuetong had the first deal, at the price of one yuan. Then more deals were reached.

The closing ceremony lasted into the evening, and we took a group photo to remember it. Before departure, the parents said gladly, "We were still worried before the event started and are now relieved to see it turn out to be such a great success."

A student's journal
The Dinosaur World of the Plumb Blossom Class
By Song Yunshu

Today we gathered in front of the gate of Longquan Lake Park for the Dinosaur World activity of our Plumb Blossom Class. It consisted of four items: drawing dinosaurs, folding paper dinosaurs, sculpting clay dinosaurs, and selling our DIY products.

While drawing the dinosaur, we needed to outline it before coloring. I drew a Stegosaurus playing on the grassland with a smile. Also on the drawing was green grass and big trees for the Stegosaurus was herbivorous.

Then Wang Yao's mother showed us how to fold paper dinosaurs. I folded a paper Stegosaurus which had no thorns on it. Guo Gengxin folded a paper Triceratops. He was the first to finish both the paper folding and the homework in the class.

The third item was clay sculpting, for which I got help from my mom. Mom sculpted the body of the dinosaur for me, and I did the four legs and stuck them to the body, all four of them.

The last thing was to sell the dinosaur products we made. I had no luck at first. Some of the customers had already bought from other students. But eventually I sold my clay dinosaur to an auntie at the price of one yuan, and I gave her the paper dinosaur for free. Then as a reward, I bought myself a popsicle. While enjoying the popsicle, I sang to myself: "Popsicle, popsicle, I love you. You are my angel."

I was a little shy when I tried to sell the clay dinosaur earlier today. I wish I could have explained its benefits to my potential customers. That would have made things much easier. I sold it anyway. It is a happy day.

So that is how I spent the day—the Dinosaur Day.

iii. Summary

There were so many highlights of the past week. I was particularly moved by the teamwork spirit of the parent committee. Yang Zishang's mother offered to buy molded dinosaur fossils from the Internet, and Xie Yuchen's mother, Wang Yao's mother, and Song Yunshu's mother offered to teach students how to draw dinosaurs, fold paper dinosaurs, and sculpt clay dinosaurs, respectively. They carefully prepared teaching materials for the class; patiently explained the physical features, dietary habits, and living environment of different types of dinosaurs; showed them how to draw, to fold, and to sculpt one by one; and taught the students to how improve their works to better represent the image of their favorite dinosaur. The students were eager to discuss with the guest teachers, with respect and awe in their eyes. In this way, the parents truly engaged in the education of students. This is the most harmonious way to cement parent–child bonds.

The closing ceremony was the most important final touch of the program. Poster making and marketing were the first challenge students had. They could draw, fold, and sculpt, but they didn't know how to make a poster or to introduce the program to others. They made faces when I asked them to go to the headmaster's office to introduce the program. So I took some students with me to see the headmaster to introduce the program. Following my footprints, the students then visited other classes in groups to introduce the program. The experience has indeed boosted their self-confidence and improved their eloquence.

At the last part when students were asked to sell their clay dinosaurs, outgoing students couldn't wait to sell their products to potential customers while introverts were struggling to make the first step, directing unsure glances to their parents from time to time. The parents were anxious, but none uttered a sound, for we had a deal. Huang Feixiang, a student from a wealthy family, never tried to sell to strangers before, and as time passed and no one stopped, he became increasingly anxious, as did his mother. But we should appreciate the opportunity. We could learn so much from strangers, indifferent or kind, such as patience and the importance of timing, which will be useful for the rest of the children's lives. This was their first lesson of life. It was a great opportunity for their growth. The dinosaur week not only taught students knowledge about dinosaurs, improved their hands-on abilities, and gave them the opportunity to make posters and sell the program to others, but also taught them the first lesson of life. They all saw their qualities improved and learned something through enjoyable activities. They said gladly, "I really like it!"

iv. Reflection

We chose to focus the science course on a special topic because this was the typical way for primary students to study science. This will give students the opportunity to do research as long as the topic interests them. The mystery of dinosaurs, which have long disappeared from the Earth, would arouse the interest and curiosity of the students. That's why we chose the topic "Into the Dinosaur World." The students spent a week learning about dinosaurs, drawing dinosaurs, folding paper dinosaurs, sculpting clay dinosaurs, and excavating molded dinosaur fossils. The abundant contents of the course revealed the mystery of the lost dinosaur empire to the students through enjoyable activities. At the end of the week, the students had more love for and scientific knowledge about dinosaurs.

The following inspirations are drawn from the dinosaur-themed science course.

First, we should increase the weight of research to the program. Ask students to propose sub-topics, divide them into groups to do the research, and guide students to produce a report on their research process or findings.

Second, we should diversify the ways to implement the science course, such as imagination, DIY, games, appreciation, contests, plantation and breeding, investigation and interview, role-play, and so on. We should create more opportunities for students to directly engage in scientific research, to raise and solve questions on their own, to experience the fun of science, to improve their capabilities of scientific research, to increase their science knowledge, and to guide them to respect evidence and raise questions.

Third, we should try developing home labs. The living room, the study, the balcony, the toilet, and so on, all the unoccupied space at home can be turned into a lab for the children to carry out all sorts of science and life experiments. Straws, a cup of water, kitchenware, and other utensils at home can become tools for experiments, and every member of the family can act as the tutor or the lab staff. We should encourage students to set up such a home lab so that every child will have the chance to engage in scientific research, make up for the limited space and time allocated to science, and extend their class education in science to outside the class.

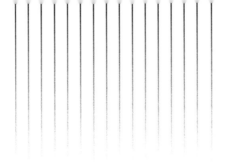

8

The New Education Experiment and Building the Digital Community

"Building the digital community" is one of the ten priority actions of the New Education Experiment. It aims to integrate online resources inside and outside schools, build an online learning community where students and teachers can learn and exchange ideas with each other, and foster their information awareness and information application abilities.

I. Connotation of "Building the Digital Community"

"Building the digital community" was one of the top five actions we proposed in the early days of the New Education Experiment. We have been, since the beginning, aware of its importance for modern society, for the education industry, for the New Education Experiment, and for the new education community.

For one thing, this action addresses the development needs of modern society. We have entered into the information society, or the so-called postindustrial society where information is the most important influencer of society and its evolvement; power, influence, and wealth tend to concentrate in the hands of people with information. The education sector is no exception. While we still organize educational activities in the traditional way and following the traditional philosophy, a quiet revolution is brewing in the education scene.

This action also meets the development needs of the New Education Experiment itself. We launched the Education Online website before the experiment, which soon rose into a spiritual homeland for new education practitioners and later a management platform for research topics of the experiment.

It is vital to build the digital community. "Community" is a bigger notion than campus. A key motive to initiate the New Education Experiment is to facilitate the sound development of more schools, teachers, and students in rural and remote areas, and create an online new education community. We propose that in today's world, with the network and digital community, you will be a step ahead of others. Online, everyone is equal and has access to the same resources as others regardless of your accumulation, financial difficulties, and geographical location. Equality is the biggest hallmark of the online world. The equal and open Internet breaks the monopoly of educational resources. Anyone who is connected to the network will have access to information and educational resources. Diannan Buyi, a webmaster of Education Online, is an ordinary primary school teacher in Simao Village in remote Yunnan Province, but he takes the pulse of the modern society via a telephone line and a computer. His life might be simple and rustic, but his mind is as sharp and cutting-edge as any urban teacher. The difference between individuals, between schools, and between regions is thus narrowed by the network.

To build a digital community, we must, first of all, strengthen the information awareness of teachers and students. Information awareness has always been a key basis for one's surviving and thriving in the digital age. Strong information awareness, the ability to tell the value of information, and the sensitivity to useful and valuable information are the preconditions for creating a digital community. Second, we must cultivate the ability to efficiently acquire information. In the age of networks, we are bombarded by much repeated information, so the ability to access information quickly and accurately is very important. Third, we shall also cultivate the initiative and ability to exchange information with others in a more effective, harmonious manner. Interpersonal communication is one of the must-have skills in modern society and has extended from offline face-to-face scenarios to online virtual scenarios. In the virtual community, communication skills are at least as important as they are in traditional society.

How do we create a digital community? We have some requirements for experimental schools. At the meeting on building the digital community held in

Jiangyan of Jiangsu Province in January 2005, I made the following suggestions. First, we should strengthen awareness of the importance of building the digital community. Second, we should increase efforts in building the digital community. Experimental schools were asked to launch their own school website as soon as possible and build it into an online platform of resources with unique characteristics of teachers, schools, and local communities. Then schools can share resources via such a platform—including teaching plans, teaching materials, and even class videos—to reduce the waste of repeated development, labor, and resources. Third, we should keep electronic records of teachers and students. All the writings of a teacher, all the homework done by a student, all the discussion between the teachers and students, and all the assessments of a teacher or student can be stored in an e-file to track the teacher's or student's personal growth. Fourth, we should establish a topic management system. Fifth, we should strengthen cyber security and promote cyber ethics. While building the digital community, we shall foster the awareness of cyber security and ethics among all the teachers and students and enhance their abilities in this regard.

To sum up, the digital community lays the foundation for the entire experiment project, serves as a key working platform, and points out the direction for educational development. How to integrate existing and create better educational resources is a question worth discussion and deliberation while we endeavor to build the digital community.

II. The Education Online Website and Building the Digital Community

The Education Online website has witnessed the evolvement of the New Education Experiment since the beginning. It gathers teachers from different parts of the country, spreads ideas of new education, and runs the experiment.

It was first launched on June 18, 2002, with Li Zhenxi, one of my doctoral students, as the chief webmaster. I wrote the following in the congratulatory message to its opening.

Here comes the Education Online, finally.

The network is a world for the young people. I have passed my prime youth, but here I am, failing to resist the temptation of network just to feel young again, to be close to the youth. I am excited but nervous about the future at the same time. I hope Education Online will gather elite educational professionals from across China to contribute to the sound development of the educational industry and the national rejuvenation of China.

For me, the ideal network should be a land of equality, free of influence hegemony or trivial formalities, but rife with only genuine feelings and thoughts.

It should be an academic utopia, serious but humorous, popular but not vulgar, and subject to ethics and laws.

It should be the common spiritual land for all, including anonymous visitors, registered users, guest speakers, and webmasters, where the principle "one for all and all for one" is happily and readily followed.

It should be a cradle of educators where constructive and sincere discussions and debates on educational topics are encouraged to inspire us and motivate us to work harder toward our dream.

It should be a medium of interaction. With the generous support of and contribution from newspapers and magazines such as *People's Political Consultative Daily*, *Teacher Expo*, *New Education*, *Teachers' Friend*, *Education Review*, and *Education Reference*, as well as publishing houses, Education Online will surely grow into an educational "Dreamworks" with sparkling wisdom and inspiration.

Education Online was instantly widely welcomed and praised by teachers. In just half a year, it received 220,000 views, with the daily average of 1,200 and the peak of 2,600, and attracted 4,506 registered users who posted nearly 10,000 threads, with nearly 10,000 posts created in total. It soon rose to be one of the top three online educational communities in China at that time. By June 2004, it had attracted 80,000 registered users and over two million visits. From "The Shockwave of a Website" published on *Jiefang Daily* and *Stories of Education Online* coedited by Zhang Jurong and others, you can see many stories about how the website promotes the personal growth of teachers.

I once tried to summarize what the Education Online website meant for me and the New Education Experiment as follows.

First, it lends me the ear to the voice of teachers. In case of any violation of existing educational policy such as making up classes and keeping students at school for too long, or any violation of teachers' rights and interests, I can be informed immediately via the website and will make sure the situation is investigated and followed up as soon as possible.

Second, I have learned about a lot of teachers on the website. At the first offline gathering of Education Online users, I surprised teachers present with my thorough knowledge of each of them. But even before the meeting, many teachers had impressed me with their dedication, educational ideals, and talents on the website. They have contributed to the success of the website, and many of them have become friends of mine.

Third, it gathers people cherishing the same educational ideal. We are living in a world where only teamwork, not individualism, can accomplish great undertakings. On Education Online I have found so many everyday heroes in the education sector. I owe to them the inspiration of many proposals I have submitted to the Two Sessions every year.

Fourth, it is a source of inspiration for my educational research. Every time I log onto the website, I can draw some inspirations from it and find some interesting topics on it. It shows me what the teachers care about, what they like, what they hate, and what changes they are experiencing in life. All this is the food for my mind and key basis for my research.

The website has played a vital role in promoting personal development of teachers. Gao Ziyang, a special-grade teacher and a long-time registered user of Education Online, once said, "Education Online has already been an indispensable part of my life. A day spent without browsing the website is a day wasted. This is an ever-green oasis, a surging fountain of life. It brings you something new every time you come. I want to thank all the friends on the website for their support for my job." Diannan Buyi, another registered user, teaches in a rural primary school, with only 12 students across the school, in Simao, Yunnan Province. He managed to reach the outside world through the network. He became the first webmaster of the Primary Education column on the website, with assistance from teacher Xiaoman, who was enthusiastic about education and known for her storytelling techniques. Together they have turned the Primary Education Forum into a highlight of the website. We are proud to have feature programs such as the composition writing series by Guan Jiangang, "Brilliant Ideas for Class Education" by Gao Ziyang, "Share Your Confusion, Share Your Ideas" by Tan Yongkang, the primary-school math salon by Xu Bin (alias "Binshan Laike"), and "Into the New Curriculum" by Zhang Xiangyang. It has attracted star teachers such as Xia Qingfeng, Xiaoqing, Zhang Yuping, Sheng Weihua, Xiqiao (Wang Wenli), Hua Zhang, Zhang Hong, and Chen Huifang. Recently famous special-grade teacher Dou Guimei has started to post on the Primary Education Forum.

Education Online hosted its first meeting of webmasters during the National Day holiday of 2002. Jiangnan Buyi and his wife traveled far from Yunnan, carrying a case of pu'er tea with them, and headed back to work immediately after the meeting ended; they didn't even have the time to enjoy the picturesque view in the south of the Yangtze River. It was a regret that I never had the chance to have a real, heart-to-heart conservation with him or do anything for his students. But after the meeting, Buyi became a star on the Education Online website, an educational hero. Soon donations and charity mail started to flood his school and hometown. For the anniversary celebration of Education Online, he wrote emotionally: "The network knows no boundaries, so does true love. Education Online is like a second home to me. It allows me to chase my dream freely, to express my ideas and feelings truthfully, to write what is in my mind candidly ... I would like to work with all of you to create more glories for the website and to pursue our shared dream—new education."

A teacher user from Wuhan said, "I turned my back to education for a while, but I was saved by Education Online and by the idea of new education. My love for Education Online is too strong to part with."

The emerging social media of Weibo, WeChat, and other social networking apps have stolen the spotlight of traditional websites and online forums, but Education Online is still active in spreading the ideas and methods of new education and managing experimental zones and schools. Meanwhile, we are considering its transformation and upgrade.

III. The New Education Online Teachers College and Building the Digital Community

The New Education Online Teachers College is a key institution of the New Education Experiment and a key practice of building the digital community. In August 2009, the New Education Institute initiated the Online Teachers College as an online learning community based on the one-year-old New Education Teachers' Reading Club. The Online Teachers College is open to educators across the country, to offer them long-term, free, professional academic guidance. I was appointed the first president of the college, and the New Education Council entrusted the teaching affairs with the New Education Research Center.

In August 2015, my second term of presidency started, and I appointed Dr. Li Zhenxi as executive vice president; Zhang Rongwei, Zhang Yong, Guo Mingxiao, and Zhang Shuoguo as vice presidents; and Lan Mei as dean of studies of the college.

Through colorful courses and sustainable efforts, we hope to help students:

1. Identify with the job—eliminate job burnout, develop strong interest in education and life, learn how to adapt oneself to the changing environment, and be active in contributing their original ideas
2. Achieve all-round professional development—strengthen comprehension ability, develop a correct understanding of new education, construct a sound knowledge system, and continue to reflect on and improve oneself
3. Deliver happy educational practices—actively apply ideas and courses of new education to real life, design relevant courses accordingly, experiment with new education with courage, and enjoy the process

I delivered a speech entitled "Fly Your Dream" at one semester-opening ceremony of the college. The text of the speech goes like this:

Dear students, teachers, and coworkers,
    Good evening.
    Today is a day worth remembering.
    On September 4 six years ago, as president of the New Education Online Teachers College, I missed the semester-opening ceremony for I was away in the mountainous areas of Guizhou on an investigation trip led by Yan Juanqi, then Vice Chairman of the National People's Congress Standing Committee.

On September 2 this year, one day before the grand military parade, our college staged our own parade too to examine our commitment to education.

In the past 15 years, we have gone through ups and downs in promoting new education.

Some schools have quit halfway, but more schools have come onboard; some teachers have left, but more have joined in.

We new education practitioners never forget our mission—to live a happy, all-around educational life.

Personally I never forget my dream—to become a new education promoter who keeps challenging oneself, seeks constant innovation, and embraces lifetime learning.

Our teachers like Li Zhenxi and Tong Xixi have done a lot of work for this new semester.

This semester, on top of all the good practices we have, we will invite more scholars from at home and abroad to exchange with students, highlight equal exchange between teachers and students, and pay more attention to online–offline integration.

I was glad to find that most of you were volunteers of our firefly volunteer program, teachers of our seed teacher program, and members of Li Zhenxi's team.

I know you must have benefited a lot from and have special feelings about new education.

I believe that in this college, you will learn from each other, make progress together, and achieve your full potential.

I am also glad to be part of you, to listen to your voice, to feel your passion for education. You are my teachers. You have been inspiring me to charge ahead.

Of course, any growth is built on concrete steps, which mean learning activities in the college.

Yesterday I received the book *Future Wise: Educating Our Children for a Changing World*, the latest book by the founder of the Project Zero of Harvard University. There is a subtitle on the Chinese cover: What is valuable learning?

This is the first question we must answer while designing courses for the Online Teachers College.

On one hand, we will continue to offer some seemingly useless and metaphysical courses such as philosophy and psychology; on the other we will call attention to what's happening in the classroom, in the school, and in the society.

I really look forward to hearing from you, to your feedback, your suggestions, and your application to give a lecture or open a course. This school is for every one of us. Here we can exchange on an equal footing and go after truth side by side.

This should be the fueling station for all of us.

In 2011, I wrote the following message to convey my expectations for the Online Teachers College:

I hope the school will continue to produce talents for the New Education Experiment, including model teachers and creators of the ideal classroom. I hope the school will explore a new path for the further education of teachers and even normal education in China and a new mode for the self-cultivation and personal growth of Chinese teachers. I hope one day the school's diploma will be more valued than the master's diploma issued by many normal universities and become the widely recognized certificate of a teacher's excellence.

As time passes, the above expectations remain solid and the path towards them becomes clearer.

The age of the Internet has given birth to many new ways of learning. The school will use more advanced technology to better serve the students.

We are working hard to create a better, easier-to-use online learning platform. But before that, let's settle for this for now. We can always make up for the poor hardware facilities with sincere communication.

We are living in a world of miracles, and I believe that our school and students will create their own miracles.

And I will always be there for you.

I am willing to continue this ever-extending journey of new education with you.

The Online Teachers College is an Internet-based, not-for-profit virtual learning community. In the spirit of new education, it is open for free to all education professionals (including teachers, teaching researchers, education researchers, and education administrators), prospective teachers, and parents interested in home education. So far, it has recruited 600 teachers.

The curriculum consists of compulsory courses, optional courses, and graduation projects. Compulsory courses include public ones and subject-specific ones. Specifically, public compulsory courses are general knowledge courses, including Pedagogy, Psychology, Philosophy, and Literature, open to all students; subject-specific compulsory courses include classics and case studies regarding the subject in question, which is Chinese for the time being, with more subjects to be covered. Existing compulsory courses include Orientation Course on New Education (by Zhu Yongxin), Development Psychology (by Lan Lan), Literary Appreciation (by Yu Lei), Home-School Co-Education (by Lan Mei), Education Writing (by Tong Xixi), and Movie Appreciation (by Li Xixi). Optional courses are divided into medium- and long-term courses and short-term courses (also known as lectures), and will be offered irregularly based on the students' needs and the specialty of guest speakers invited. Existing optional courses include Headmaster Management (by Li Zhenxi), Life Narration Play (by Guo Mingxiao), From Kindergartens to Primary Schools (by Hu Zhiyuan), Understanding Mathematics (by Zhang Yong), Child Literature (by Peng Xuejun), and The History of Literary Education (by Huang Yaohong). After finishing all the required courses, students are asked to design and deliver a course in their school by applying what they have learned, take notes, and make an analysis, and submit the report of the graduation project to the expert committee of the Online Teachers College for review and defense.

All the teaching and learning activities are conducted on the Education Online website, QQ, and WeChat (public account: xjywlsfxy). The distribution and collection of educational resources and homework and the instant discussions on a given topic all take place in writing or by voice on the Internet. The classes are normally given for two hours in the evening, but the duration varies from class to class.

Students can choose the courses they want, and then the affairs management division will make adjustments when necessary. Each compulsory course is worth ten credit points, each medium- and long-term optional course five credit points, and each short-term course, or lecture, two credit points per semester. Each student must have at least 120 credit points in order to graduate. To guarantee the study effect, generally each student should take at least one compulsory course, and no more than three compulsory and optional courses in total for each semester; but for full-time students, each must take no more than four courses in each semester, including at least one compulsory course. Those who have taken all the required courses, passed all the exams, and defended their graduation project will be allowed to graduate. Students who don't have enough credit points but have completed the graduation project in advance can also apply for defense. The certificate of graduation issued is honorary and for certification only.

The recruitment is application based. Interested students need to fill in and submit the application form, register on the Education Online website, open their own personal thread, and submit a piece of writing of no less than 3,000 Chinese characters to introduce their own reading history.

The Online Teachers College is an original attempt to cultivate teachers and seed teachers via a network. The training is not diploma-oriented but directly relevant to actual educational life, producing considerable effects and receiving much attention from the education sector.

IV. Exploration of Future Schools and Building the Digital Community

Since we proposed to build the digital community in 2000, we new education practitioners have been deliberating on educational reform and school development in the age of networks. I put forth the idea of future schools at the end of 2015 and suggested the following trends in education.

First, today's schools will evolve into learning centers in the future. Traditional schools will be replaced by learning centers. People won't have to go to school as scheduled every day and take courses as required. Second, teaching will be replaced by learning, and today's teaching activities will evolve into student-oriented learning activities. Third, today's teachers will become partners or learning assistants of students. Fourth, today's classrooms will become learning rooms where students study. Fifth, today's standardized education will become customized and personalized. Traditional school education delivered and assessed according to unified standards will be customized and personalized.

Steve Jobs once asked a famous question about educational reform: "Given so much input into information technology for education, how come we haven't seen the same effect as in areas of production and distribution?" In September 2011, then U.S. Secretary of Education Arne Duncan blamed it on "the lack of structural changes to education." The application of information technology to education has gone through three stages: changes to instruments and technology, changes to the teaching mode, and eventually possible changes to school forms.

Then how do we change the form of schools against the backdrop of Internet? I think the following three points should be considered.

First, we should strive to create a student-centered educational community. The current educational system as a whole is built on the legacy of the Industrial Revolution, advocates massive education, and puts efficiency above everything else, with knowledge dissemination as its chief mission. As long as all this remains the same, no true changes will occur to education. We must shift the focus from knowledge to students. Schools demand you to show up every morning on time no matter where you live and to learn the same thing as other students no matter if you like it or not. This must change. I think in the future, no matter where you are, in cities or villages, you won't have to go to school at the required time every day. It will be unnecessary because you can study at home.

We should establish the home schooling system in China as soon as possible. Why can't children study at home or in libraries? Why do we have to force children of different learning experiences, interest, and habits to come to the same classroom? They can learn via the network, in groups, or on their own. Each student can have his own curriculum whose contents are subject to changes when necessary. In the future, no matter where you are, in an urban or rural school, you won't have to take courses as required; instead, you can choose courses that you find interesting or practical. Learning will become autonomous, networked, and collaborative on a massive scale. We won't have to help students create a complete knowledge structure. With the primary knowledge structure, students may, through self-directed learning, construct their own personalized structure that serves his or her personal needs. The current knowledge structure we try to feed them with is too huge and difficult for the majority of students. We need to break the mode. The establishment of basic requirements will suffice. Credits, diplomas, and schools won't matter any longer in the future. What really matters is what you have learned, what you have shared, what you have constructed, and what you have created.

Second, we should develop national standards on education and a national repository of educational resources. The top priority is to establish national standards on education. Why? It's because the changes to the learning method will raise higher demands for learning content. The freer, the more customized and personalized education is, the more urgent it is for us to integrate national resources and establish efficient, high-quality learning centers. What is education? It is a process where culture is selected and passed down. Its top mission is to pass down the values cherished by our country and people. The government is responsible for making the choice and therefore must develop national standards on it. The most important thing is that they must not be developed by a handful; they should be more scientific, more personalized, and have a bottom line. The education we provide now is too deep and hard in contents, and many of the educational problems we encounter are rooted in the standards we have.

Then when the standards are set, what resources will we provide? The existing way of resource supply is problematic too. Where are the top resources? They are like a needle in a haystack. How do we mobilize the whole country to integrate the best educational resources in the world? There are numerous massive open online courses such as NetEase OpenCourse and those offered by universities, but we don't have a national platform to integrate them. I think this is what we need: a national platform that gathers all the best educational resources in the world and is open to all for free with just one click. Meanwhile, we should also integrate all the high-quality resources developed by nongovernmental educational organizations and even individuals through government purchase. Schools are wasting limited input developing their own education platform, education center, and courseware. That's why the government should step in to organize task forces, integrate resources with the help of advanced network technology, and breathe life into idle resources and rigid courses.

Third, we should create an Internet-based education and exam evaluation system. What is good education? How is the knowledge system truly mastered? Which talents do we really need? How do we test and assess the learning effect? To answer these questions, we need to advance the reform through assessment. Evaluation and exam are the weather vane for the reform, but the current evaluation system is too outdated. There is no single Chinese university that is truly capable of measuring talents. What makes a good student? No principal in China is confident enough to give his own answer. We say the current evaluation mechanism is problematic because it is designed not for improvement, but for labeling, for selection, and for elimination. Therefore, it must be changed.

In the future, evaluation will no longer be for differentiation, but for improvement. In the early stage of learning, we can use big data to automatically record the learning process of each student as the basis for future evaluation. While tracking the process, we should be able to identify the weakness and help overcome it in a timely manner. Meanwhile, future exams and evaluation will focus more on a student's practical skills instead of his educational background. Changes might occur to higher education too. In the future, no matter where you go to college, as long as you pass the scientific, rigid, and internationally recognized evaluation in certain specialty, you will be able to land a job with the certification. In that case, what changes will happen to education? In the future, the competition might not be about school brands, but course brands. The Internet has made it possible for a single course to be taken by over one million students at the same time. The quality of a school will be primarily reflected in the quality of its courses.

In summary, in today's world where the Internet is redefining everything, we can see a new educational scene and future schools on the horizon. Following the attempts with the Education Online website and the Online Teachers College, the New Education Experiment will continue to explore the creation of a digital community and pave the way for future education.

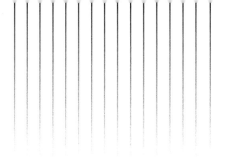

9

The New Education Experiment and the One Thing per Month Initiative

From the very beginning, the new education experiment has attached great importance to the fostering of habits. Among the five ideas that the new education experiment has been advocating since the beginning of the twenty-first century is the idea of teaching things that will benefit students' whole life. Knowledge and skills are surely things that bring benefits to students, but here by stressing "things that will benefit students' whole life," we are aiming at habits that have the most profound influence on a person's life. Guided by this idea, the new education experiment has launched the One Thing per Month initiative. Efforts to foster the 12 primary habits and 36 second-layer habits have yielded concrete results. Students and teachers equipped with the core habits are seeing an increasingly vigorous educational life.

I. The Launch of the One Thing per Month Initiative Under the New Education Experiment Framework

Born against the backdrop of the knowledge economy and the information society, the new education experiment has clearly pronounced its adherence to the action philosophy and field spirit from the very start. Setting the goals of new education, we had been looking around for an easily understood way to convey the idea of "teaching things that will benefit students' whole life" before "habits" hit us as what accurately captured the values of the times. Instead of the internal and largely intangible "competences," we have chosen to focus on the more observable "habits" that can be acquired and internalized through practical courses and programs such as the One Thing per Month initiative.

The first annual symposium of the New Education Experiment held in July 2003 became an initial landmark as we continued to promote the fostering of habits among students. In that symposium, we announced "faith, hope, love, learning, thinking, and perseverance" as the six "useful things" besides knowledge and skills that would help students succeed.

Starting in 2006, a doctoral program of Suzhou University dedicated about a year to the issue of identifying the most important and crucial habits to a person's success in study, work, and life, and our discussions added further insights to our exploration.

In 2007, we formerly launched the One Thing per Month initiative, a new education program mainly aimed at fostering good habits, and Haimen New Education Experiment Zone undertook the initial pilot program.

In March 2007, Haimen Experiment Zone organized a promotion meeting in Sanchang Primary School themed "education toward the fostering of good habits." Dr. Xu Xinhai shared his understanding of the Regional Action Plan for Good Habits Oriented Education and announced the roadmap for promoting the One Thing per Month initiative in the region.

Similar meetings were held in the Primary School Affiliated to Haian Normal College in 2008 and Sanxing Primary School in 2009 that contributed to a well-considered action plan for the One Thing per Month Initiative.

In 2009, Tianjin Education Press published *Twelve Good Habits that Benefit Your Whole Life: Program Manual for New Education Experiment's One Thing per Month Initiative*. This book, complied by Haimen Experiment Zone, was readily embraced by new education experiment zones and schools. In the book, the 12 habits advocated by the initiative were embodied in 12 activities throughout the 12 months of the year: frugality (eating) for January, rules (walking) for February, public welfare (planting trees) for March, nature (outing) for April, labor (sweeping the floor) for May, art (singing) for June, fitness (playing ball games) for July, communication (smiling) for August, knowledge (reading) for September, gratitude (writing letters home) for October, confidence (public speaking) for November, and self-reflection (diary) for December.

Figure 9.1   New Education's One Thing per Month Initiative: 12 Primary Habits and 36 Second-Layer Habits

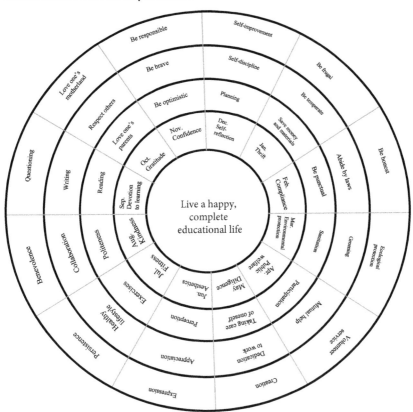

Based on the experience of Haimen and other experiment zones and drawing on the findings of domestic and international studies on core competencies, we have fine-tuned the 12 habits in recent years and proceeded to develop 36 second-layer habits, as detailed in Figure 9.1.

The One Thing per Month initiative has the following features:

First, it is guided by unique educational values. The initiative never aims at randomly acquired habits, but habits that lead to a happy and all-around educational life as well as the maturity of a person's character. Its integrative forces complete the educational life of teachers and students once fragmented by disciplines and subjects. The implementation of the initiative itself forms part of a happy educational life. The 12 habits that it advocates correspond to the 12 essential qualities that make a person "complete." It is only natural that such "complete persons" will ultimately create and embrace a most "happy and complete life." Guided by these values, we give special importance to personal growth, social interactions, and artistic attainment when developing the 12 habits. They not only serve to prolong our natural life, expand our social life, and elevate our spiritual life, but also correspond to the national call for fostering core competencies among citizens.

Second, it represents a unique action pattern to translate the theories of new education into practice. Although it is no more than a program, it manifests through every specific action, the goal of new education to help every child "live a most happy and all-around educational life" and one of the five principal ideas of "teaching things that will benefit students' whole life." Happiness is closely tied to our daily work and life, and the various habits acquired in our work and life. The core habits acquired in childhood will affect what person we grow up to be and what life we are going to live. We have carefully selected the theme, the primary habit, the overall goal, and the second-layer habits for each month, making them both operational and practical. We also ensure that it not only covers the 15 years of a student's educational life but also lays a solid foundation for lifelong learning.

Lastly, it resonates with the rhythm of a child's school and family life. The initiative is designed to keep pace with students' childhood life trajectory. The yearly learning plan unfolds around monthly themes including those for summer and winter vacations and integrates family education and school activities. For example, January marks the beginning of a new year and promises the start of the winter vacation and the advent of the Spring Festival. As students are expected to engage in more family gatherings and feasts in this month, we choose "thrift" as the theme for January, advocating a frugal lifestyle manifested through the saving of food. As the winter vacation often falls in February and students are most likely to spend this month traveling, "obeying rules" is the natural theme for the second month of the year. Learning to obey traffic rules is the first step toward becoming a rule-abiding member of society equipped with the spirit of contract. September is when the new semester begins. September 28 is the birthday of Confucius and the Reading Day for new education experiment schools. We choose "devotion to learning" as the theme for September to highlight the importance of developing a love for books in early childhood.

The identification of each of the 12 primary habits also follows the rules governing the physical and spiritual growth of students. Different development stages are matched with second-layer habits of different levels of importance and complexity. For example, in order to realize the overall goal of becoming "frugal," students have to first become saving (goal for lower grades), then temperate (goal for middle grades), and ultimately thrifty (goal for higher grades). Similarly, the overall goal of "diligence" is only achieved through a gradual ascension from "taking care of oneself" through "dedicating oneself to work" to "dedicating to creative activities." The three-step formula is also applicable in the case of fostering a love for "public welfare" as it respectively stresses "participation," "mutual help," and "volunteer service."

Therefore, the action plan of the One Thing per Month initiative is best implemented through lessons and activities that are developed around the 12 primary habits and follow the rules governing children's growth. Ideally, such lessons and activities should be rich in content and diverse in forms and correspond to the 12 months of a complete school year. However, as schools and classes may start from different stages and thus require different time frameworks to foster such habits, it is absolutely feasible for them to devote a certain period of time to a specific "thing," or habit, with full attention and targeted measures.

The One Thing per Month initiative, with its carefully selected monthly themes and skillfully arranged primary and second-layer habits covering every aspect of student's family and school life and following closely all educations rules, endeavors to help students foster habits, improve personality, and ultimately live a happy and complete life through the silent but powerful influence of education.

II. The Connotation and Procedure of Promoting the One Thing per Month Initiative Under the New Education Framework

As one of the ten major actions of new education experiment, the One Thing per Month initiative represents an innovative and unique approach toward habit fostering. It does not strive to replace habit fostering but stands as a most important tool for its realization. It provides an ideal platform for moral education and an essential path toward building the ideal classroom.

The One Thing per Month initiative is also a teaching program consisting of a variety of courses, and every monthly theme forms a small self-contained universe. It is always dynamic, constantly being implemented, re-created, enriched, and improved. It follows the rules governing students' physical and spiritual growth, keeps pace with the rhythm of school and family life, and combines classroom and extracurricular activities. It integrates all school events from class meetings to celebrations and all school resources. Every month, it sponsors a clearly themed educational event aimed at a useful habit. Guided by the goal of helping students develop their personality and live an all-around and happy educational life, it teaches students things that will benefit the rest of their life one by one, step by step.

i. The Connotation of the One Thing per Month Initiative

The program mainly develops around four items, namely, primary habit, overall goal, second-layer habits, and model activity. Primary habit refers to the habit aimed to foster, overall goal means the personal quality aimed to cultivate through the fostering of the primary habit, secondary habits are hierarchically organized to reflect the increasing difficulty in their attainment, and the model activity forms the starting point for each age group. One by one, one thing follows another, and life will reward you with the good habits and precious qualities as promised (see Table 9.1).

Table 9.1 New Education's One Thing per Month Initiative: 12 Primary Habits and 36 Second-Layer Habits

Month	One Thing per Month	Primary Habit	Second-Layer Habits	Model Activity
January	Be thrifty	Be saving and frugal	Be frugal	Let's learn how to eat a meal!
			Be temperate	Let's only play when allowed to!
			Be thrifty	Let's learn to cherish old things!
February	Obey rules	Adhere to principles	Be punctual	Let's never be late for school!
			Be law-abiding	Let's never run a red light!
			Be honest	Let's never tell lies to cover our mistakes!
March	Environment protection	Protect our environment	Mind personal hygiene	Let's be clean and tidy!
			Conserve the greenery	Let's plant trees!
			Think ecologically	Let's learn to classify garbage!
April	Public welfare	Do good things	Participate	Let's participate in one public welfare program!
			Help each other	Let's all do one good thing!
			Volunteer	Let's be volunteer organizers!
May	Diligence	Enjoy one's work	Take care of oneself	Let's learn how to clean the floor!
			Dedicate oneself to one's work	Let's fulfill our duties with devotion!
			Create	Let's make models!
June	Aesthetics	Understand art	Feel	Let's learn a song!
			Appreciate	Let's appreciate a painting!
			Perform	Let's give a performance!

116

July	Fitness	Love life	Sports	Let's play ball games!
			Health	Let's follow a healthy daily schedule!
			Perseverance	Let's jog every day!
August	Friendliness	Get along with others	Be polite	Let's learn to behave politely!
			Cooperate	Let's be good friends!
			Love all	Let's get to know one nation (country)!
September	Devotion to learning	Enjoy learning new knowledge	Read	Let's read happily!
			Write	Let's stay focused while thinking!
			Question	Let's challenge masters!
October	Gratitude	Have a loving heart	Love our parents	Let's write a letter to our parents!
			Respect others	Let's do something nice for our friends and teachers!
			Love our country	List ten reasons why we should love our country!
November	Confidence	"I can do it!"	Be optimistic	Let's not get angry when wronged by others!
			Be brave	Let's give a public speech!
			Commit oneself	Let's volunteer for a difficult task!
December	Self-reflection	Be reflective	Plan	Let's make plans!
			Self-discipline	Let's keep track of our life!
			Self-improve	Let's brave difficulties!

Thrift is the theme for January, and it aims to make students save and be frugal. The second-layer habits proceed from saving, through temperate to thrifty. Thrift makes people store and accumulate, prepares them against the odds in the future, and turns the world into a gold mine. As the Chinese classic *Master Chu's Homilies for Families* teaches, "The growing of rice and of grain/ Think on whenever you dine; Remember how silk is obtained/Which keeps you warm and looks fine." When thrift becomes a habit, we possess a virtual treasure chest. Meanwhile, a contented mind is the greatest blessing in the world and too much desire blocks the way to inner peace and happiness. A thrifty person works hard but wants little. He is easily content and most likely to find happiness. Model activities for January may include "Let's learn how to eat a meal!" "Let's only play when allowed to!" and "Let's learn to cherish old things!" When we eat, learn to cherish the food. When we play, we learn to cherish things around us. Start from these small things, and we will gradually foster a thrifty habit and a simple lifestyle, which will benefit us for the rest of our life.

Obeying rules is the theme for February, and the overall goal is adhering to principles. The second-layer habits proceed from punctual, through law-abiding, to honest. We are living in a world governed by rules. Rules ensure the order of the world, form the contracts for survival and development among people, and integrate rights, responsibilities, and obligations. Rules are our ultimate shelter against disorder and intimate guard for a harmonious life. A social person must play by the rules to which everyone has consented. People who dismiss rules may get some extra advantages for the time being, but as cleverness can backfire, eventually they will be punished by rules and discarded by the times. From being punctual to meetings and appointments and abiding by the law in daily life to being honest in society, rules make us trusted and credible human beings. The failure to be punctual wastes others' lives. The failure to abide by the law turns a person into a broken kite that plunges to the ground after a short madness. The failure to be honest erodes a person's reputation and makes him or her invisible to others. Therefore, obeying rules is a very important habit and the highest requirement is to remain prudent in privacy. Rules are inside us and should always be obeyed, with or without supervision. Model activities for February may include "Let's never be late for school!" "Let's never run a red light!" and "Let's never tell lies to cover our mistakes!" Start from these small things, and we will foster a respect for rules and a habit to obey rules.

In March, we focus on environmental protection and identify "protecting our environment" as the overall goal. The second-layer habits proceed from paying attention to personal hygiene, through conserving the greenery, to thinking ecologically. Many festivals that fall in March are related to environmental protection. In March, we celebrate Youth Volunteer Service Day on the fifth day, Mother River Protection Day on the ninth, Chinese Tree Planting Day on the twelfth, World Forest Day and World Sleep Day on the twenty-first, World Water Day on the twenty-second, World Meteorological Day on the twenty-third, and World Tuberculosis Day on the twenty-fourth. The richness of the theme allows us much freedom to develop our program, from the fostering of personal hygiene habits to raising the awareness of natural protection, from cherishing our ecosystem to understanding the mutual dependence between nature and mankind. Everyone is unique, and paying attention to personal hygiene is the first step toward protecting oneself. Diversity is the very reason why this world exists and operates in a most beautiful way. When we cherish our environment, we are protecting our own home. When we take care of animals and plants, we are caring for humankind. When environmental protection becomes a habit, we are seeing the world and all its creatures as our equals and enjoying the stunning beauty of nature with a true and peaceful mind. Model activities may include "Let's be clean and tidy!" "Let's plant trees!" and "Let's learn to classify garbage!" Students are expected to become pro-environmental in the long run.

Public welfare is the theme for April, and the overall goal is doing good things. The second-layer habits proceed from participating, through helping each other, to volunteering. Public welfare, simply put, can be anything good for the public. When we say "all for one and one for all," we are talking about active participation, cooperation, and even sacrifice, all the things that make good thrive and spread happiness. The magic is that happiness only increases when shared by more. Originally, "public welfare" was only a sub-theme for March. When we were reviewing the master report, some experts pointed out that volunteer spirit and public welfare were so important that they should constitute a separate theme, one that stood side by side with environmental protection rather than fell under it. That is why we replaced the theme of "embracing nature through a spring outing" with "being a volunteer." Like March, April sees quite a number of festivals. Besides the Pure Brightness Festival (Qingming Festival), people celebrate International Children's Book Day on April 2, World Health Day on April 7, Earth Day on April 22, World Book and Copyright Day (or World Reading Day) on April 23, China Prophylactic Vaccination Day on April 25, National Traffic Safety Reflection Day on April 30, and World Children's Day on the fourth Sunday of April. Skillfully using and integrating resources afforded by these festivals will make our education more effective and practical. For example, we may organize reading events on World Reading Day to help students better understand the meaning of public good. Model activities may include "Let's participate in one public welfare program!" "Let's all do one good thing!" and "Let's be volunteer organizers!" Good things are never too small to matter. Let's start from here and now!

Diligence is the theme for May, and the overall goal is enjoying one's work. The second-layer habits proceed from taking care of oneself, through dedicating to one's work, to being creative. May begins with the International Labor Day. We believe that a loving parent and an understanding teacher should always let their children do their own things and take part in proper physical labor. In a sense, depriving children of their labor rights is blocking their way to growth. The greatest act of love is letting go. Let children take care of themselves, let them practice, and let them become independent! I would like to quote an anecdote about Chen Fan, a celebrity of the Eastern Han Dynasty. As a teenager, Chen Fan only wanted to do "big things." One day, his friend Xue Qin paid him a visit. Shocked by his filthy and rubbish-strewn courtyard, Xue Qin asked, "Why don't you sweep the floor and clean the courtyard before receiving the guests?" Chen Fan replied, "A great man should aim high and the world is his platform. Why should I be restrained to a courtyard?" Xue Qin retorted, "If you don't clean your own courtyard, how can you settle the world?" That struck Chen Fan speechless. From small beginnings come great things, and all great men start with simple things like cleaning one's own courtyard. Zeng Guofan, statesman, military general, and Confucian scholar of the late Qing dynasty, once said, "Diligence is the basis of all virtues and the source of all attainments." As the *Book of Changes* teaches, "As heaven maintains vigor through movements, a gentle man should constantly strive for self-perfection." Dedication to one's work and self-improvement is a most valuable virtue of the Chinese nation. Participating in physical labor teaches us not only craftsmanship and dedication, but also the importance of understanding and respecting others, thus paving the way for an independent life. The more capable you are, the more likely you are to find in hard work ultimate happiness, the source of inspiration, and the motivation for perfection. Model activities may include "Let's learn how to clean the floor!" "Let's fulfill our duties with devotion!" and "Let's make models!" Students are expected to develop a love for physical labor and through a desire to make the best of their life.

Aesthetics is the theme for June, and the overall goal is understanding art. The second-layer habits proceed from feeling, through appreciation, to performance. June is a month for children and art. The month begins with International Children's Day and the International Children's Film Festival (on June 1) and ends with the World Festival of Youth and Students (on June 30). That's why we decided to dedicate the whole month of June to art education every year. Through organized events, we are hoping that our students will learn to play one or two musical instruments, sing several songs that will accompany them for the rest of their life, and most importantly, form their own aesthetic system. Making every child artistic has always been a goal of new education. However, that does not mean every child has to become an artist. Rather, we are looking for children who love and appreciate art. A life accompanied by art is rich and fulfilled. Learn to enjoy art and appreciate beauty, and such a life can be our ultimate aspiration. Get close to different forms of art, and you will better find beauty and feel its charm. A numb mind turns a blind eye to beauty and deprives life of its chance to see and create art. A sharp mind captures beauty in the subtlest form and urges life to share and re-create. Model activities may include "Let's learn a song!" "Let's appreciate a painting!" and "Let's give a performance!" Art decorates our life, nurtures our soul, and integrates internal and external beauty.

Fitness is the theme for July, and the overall goal is loving life. The second-layer habits proceed from doing sports, through staying healthy, to fostering perseverance. The long summer vacation starts in July. How to make the best of it? We suggest students spending 30 minutes to an hour doing sports every day so that it becomes an interest, a habit, and an ability. Nowadays, more and more people are saying that health is like the leading digit, one, in a really big number and everything else is like the zero behind it. Without the one, the number instantly collapses to zero. Doing sports and keeping fit lays the foundation for a beautiful life. Abundant research findings prove that mind and body are inseparable. Exercise not only builds the body, but also strengthens the will. A strong body is always accompanied by a strong mind. Sports increase our flexibility, endurance, speed, and perseverance; make us braver and more responsive; and inspire us to observe rules more closely. Group sports have the additional benefits of fostering team spirit and a respect for collective good. Exercise should become a lifelong habit, and it will continue to bring benefits to our body and mind. Model activities for July may include "Let's play ball games!" "Let's follow a healthy daily schedule!" and "Let's jog every day!" Through a rich variety of fitness and sports programs, we are helping students foster a spirit of perseverance.

Friendliness is the theme for August, and the overall goal is getting along with others. The second-layer habits proceed from being polite, through being cooperative, to loving all. In August, students spend their summer vacation away from school. Some go on vacation with their parents, some visit relatives or friends, and others take part in various community activities. That means they will have a better opportunity to interact with others and learn about the society. Therefore, August is a most suitable time for students to learn some interpersonal skills. Humans are social by nature. We are born with an inherent need to communicate with and understand others. Friendliness brings two strangers close and turns hopes into reality. It is the most beautiful smile we can wear and the most nourishing land where we can plant the seeds of hope. In modern society, the division of labor turns people into strangers. Friendliness is the bridge that connects people of different races and nations and makes the world a warm place to live in. When we greet others with a smile, readily offer a helping hand, take a different perspective, and respect other people's habits, privacy, and way of thinking, we are being friendly. When we know how to communicate, cooperate, and avoid embarrassing others, we are living a friendly life. These are also things we want to teach our students in August. Model activities for August may include "Let's learn to behave politely!" "Let's be good friends!" and "Let's get to know one nation (country)!" Interpersonal skills are a most important quality and can be the source of lifelong happiness.

Devotion to learning is the theme for September, and the overall goal is enjoying learning knowledge. The second-layer habits proceed from reading, through writing, to questioning. September ushers in the golden season of autumn and marks the beginning of a new semester. In this month, students embark on a new journey of hope and promise. Creating a "Campus with the Fragrance of Books" has always been a most important action of new education. On the twenty-eighth day of this month, we celebrate the birthday of Confucius, the great philosopher and cultural and spiritual symbol of the Chinese nation whose dedication to learning has inspired generations of the Chinese people to strive for self-perfection. In this month, the journey of learning continues, with new hope sowed and new harvest expected. Learning is an inherent power. Children are curious by nature and always eager to learn. However, only through thinking and reflection can we turn lessons of books and life into wisdom that takes root in and continues to nurture our life. Modern society calls for lifelong learning, and reading is a most direct means to that end. September is only the beginning. We hope that the fragrance of books continues to fill the life of our students, through "morning recital, noon reading, and evening reflection." Children are to read on their own, under the professional guidance of teachers, and in the company of family members. Model activities for September may include "Let's read happily!" "Let's stay focused when thinking!" and "Let's challenge masters!" Learners conquer all. Happiness is ensured when learning becomes a way of life.

Gratitude is the theme for October, and the overall goal is a loving heart. The second-layer habits proceed from loving our parents, through respecting others, to loving our country. In our early days, we are helpless babies whose very survival depends on the kindness of others, especially our family members. In our veins runs the blood of our parents, our grandparents, our family, and ultimately our nation. We would not have come to this world without them. Besides family members, there are many other people that we should be grateful to. Our life depends on the support of others. Thanks to the hard work of peasants, workers, and many other providers, we can have food, clothing, housing, and access to transportation. With its blue sky and white clouds, brooks and oceans, trees and flowers, nature shelters us, feeds us, and nourishes us. As students, we need the help of teachers and classmates. As employees, we are warmed by the kindness of our managers and colleagues. The caring hand of a friend leads us out of loneliness. For all this, we should be grateful. For all this, we should give back. Many festivals that fall in October are related to gratitude. The first day of this month is our National Day, the fourth day World Animal Day, the sixth day the International Day of Older Persons, and the thirteenth day World Teachers' Day. Two Chinese traditional festivals, the Mid-Autumn Festival and the Double Ninth Festival, often fall in October. Mid-Autumn Day, observed on the fifteenth day of the eighth month of the lunar calendar, is a time for family reunion, while Double Ninth Day, observed on the ninth day of the ninth month of the lunar calendar, is an opportunity to care for and appreciate the elderly. For Chinese, the two festivals bear special significance. That's why we choose October as the month for gratitude, though people in western countries usually celebrate Thanksgiving Day in November. Through proper ways, we should express our gratitude to our parents for raising us, to our teachers for enlightening us, and to others for helping us. We should also thank nature for nourishing us, society for supporting us, and our motherland for sheltering us. Model activities for October may include "Let's write a letter to our parents!" "Let's do something nice for our friends and teachers!" and "List ten reasons why we should love our country!" Expressing gratitude to others is the first step toward becoming a responsible person.

Confidence is the theme for November, and the overall goal is "I can do it." The second-layer habits proceed from optimism, through bravery, to commitment. Confidence makes trivial great and ordinary magnificent. Confidence saves people and braves them against adversity. An optimistic person generates confidence, a brave person tests confidence, and a responsible person showcases confidence. Speaking in public is a most useful way to build confidence. Fostering eloquence is one of the ten major actions of new education. Here, we are especially concerned with the qualities behind a confidently delivered public lecture such patience, optimism, courage, and commitment. Expressing oneself and communicating with others are two of the most important qualities that influence our life. Some people say that language has the power to conquer the human mind, which is the most complicated thing in the world. Confidence, courage, and commitment makes a successful speaker. Eloquence is always tied with confidence. Those who dare to have their voice heard tend to have higher confidence. That is why we suggest that confidence is in a certain sense built through the fostering of eloquence. Model activities may include "Let's not get angry when wronged by others!" "Let's give a public speech!" and "Let's volunteer for a difficult task!" Like sunshine, confidence always sheds light on our way forward.

Self-reflection is the theme for December, and the overall goal is being reflective. The second-layer habits proceed from planning, through exercising self-discipline, to improving oneself. Some people say that life is not the days that have passed but the days we will remember. Others say that the unexamined life is not worth living. Whatever the case, there is no doubt that the last month of the year should be a time for self-reflection. A person who makes plans and makes good use of his or her time cannot drift along. A person who keeps track of his or her life, work, study, and thoughts, who continues to reflect on the gains and losses, and who listens to his or her own voice and communicates with his or her soul will have a rich inner world. In ancient times, people kept a diary to "record important things, current events, and personal thoughts." It was also a most effective way to reflect on the past day. Keeping a diary is more than recording. It is about self-education, reflection, and examination. Keep track of your life and do not let a day pass unrecorded, and tenacity and perseverance will become your virtue. The best education is self-education, an education with no teachers. A person who always makes plans, reflects, and exercises self-discipline will stand on his or her own feet and laugh in the face of difficulties and challenges. Model activities may include "Let's make plans!" "Let's keep track of our life!" and "Let's brave difficulties!" Teachers and students are expected to become more self-reflective and better equipped to draw lessons from failures and experience from successes, which is crucial for continued personal growth.

ii. The Procedure of the One Thing per Month Initiative

After years of practice, we have developed a standard procedure of the One Thing per Month Initiative. A five-step approach is applied to each monthly theme.

First, launch the monthly themed event in a formal way. Ceremonies to mark the beginning of a new semester or an important festival, regular class meetings in the morning, and flag-raising ceremonies all provide ideal opportunities to formally announce the launch of the monthly themed event, as rituals add a sense of solemnity to the event. Zhengda Primary School of Haimen set a good example when it organized a special ceremony on April 30 to launch the monthly event named "Starlight Coin and Start Your Business." The event was aimed to help students develop a love for work and a habit of diligence. The ceremony also witnessed the establishment of the Starlight Bank, the Starlight Auction House, and the Starlight Venture Store. In front of all the teachers and students gathered in the school gymnasium, the school principal and vice principal presented business licenses to the president of the Starlight Bank, the auctioneer of the Starlight Auction House, and the salesperson of the Starlight Venture Store. Students were also briefed on the projects on the list and the way to register them.

Second, bring meaning to students through deep reading. Reading makes us wiser and nurtures our taste. Theme-specific deep reading helps teachers and students better understand the connotation, cultural background, and significance of a monthly themed event and encourages us to take active action to participate in it.

The key lies in finding the right materials that match students' cognitive and reading competences and are suitable for school and home reading activities. Recommendations should take into consideration the overall aim of a themed event and different needs of students in different grades. For preschool children and students in the first and second grades of primary school, nursery rhymes, children's songs, and short stories are good choices. Students may be encouraged to read whole books as they enter higher grades. While third- and fourth-grade students are old enough for poetry, their seniors can start trying ancient classics.

The *New Education Morning Recital Series*, edited by the New Education Research Institute, has set a good example. For each theme, it selects poems and other classic reading materials that suit different age groups. The New-Style Reading Institute under the New Education Research Institute launched the *Basic Book List for Children in China*, the *Basic Book List for Primary School Students in China*, the *Basic Book List for Junior High School Students in China*, and the *Basic Book List for Senior High School Students in China*, providing valuable references for children at different ages to find the most suitable books.

Meanwhile, the New-Style Parents Institute under the New Education Institute launched a film course, and a total of 72 films were recommended under different themes of the One Thing per Month initiative. The fruit of the course was a published collection titled *Fostering Good Habits Through 36 Film Lectures*. The course draws on the artistic appeal of a film and utilizes the interaction between the film, the audience, and the targeted habit to bring to students the importance of the habit and help them better internalize such habits. Wang Yan, deputy head of the project team of the film course and teacher of Huai' an Tianjin Road Primary School of Jiangsu Province, organized a parent–child film viewing event in 2014. *The Secret of the Magic Gourd*, the film chosen for that occasion, attracted more than 800 viewers, mostly students and their parents, to the school lecture hall. Unlike the excitement of the children, which was only too natural, the solemn thoughtfulness of their parents was unexpected. Afterwards, parents shared their reflections on the old chattering way of parenting through face-to-face and online discussions.

In addition to "morning recital, noon reading, and evening reflection," deep reading in the classroom is another effective way to make full use of the weekly reading class and students' extracurricular time. Together, the teacher and students read a story, an article, or a book and share their thoughts in regular class meetings. This way of deep reading helps bring to students the essence of books.

Parent–child reading can also follow monthly themes. Through the parents' school, weekly letters to parents, and the School Open Day, the school can recommend books to parents for parent–child reading. After reading, students are encouraged to record and share their thoughts through personal blogs, class blogs and journals, school newspapers and journals, and other easily accessible platforms.

Third, take action and let students practice. By name, One Thing per Month is an action-oriented initiative. However, it should be stressed that all our actions should fit into their respective theme and course in a most natural manner. Fragmentation and separation are never our aim. These actions should not only enlighten classroom activities, but also help students understand and acquire their needed habits. Therefore, designers should always bear in mind the requirements of student participation, relevance, repeatable process, and effectiveness. We should not only create the conditions and atmosphere for students to participate and practice, but also encourage and help students to foster the behavior habits during the process. Through action and practice, students will gradually form the habits that enable them to develop their personality and live a happy and complete life.

Take Changshou District No.1 Experimental Primary School of Chongqing for example. Under the monthly theme of "gratitude," it launched a series of activities that suited the physical and mental development of its students. The school collected the ideas of the students and developed the "Small Actions Plan." Students were required to say goodbye to their family when leaving for school in the morning, greet their elders or give them a hug whenever they met, carry their own schoolbag on the way home from school, and do at least one household chore every day. "Family Bookkeeping" was another class-based program designed to bring students closer to their family. Students were asked to write down all the expenses that had been paid for them since their birth, together with their parents. It proved an effective way to show students the devotion and love of their parents in raising them. "A Loving World" brought students, parents, and teachers, together with their greetings and souvenirs, to the nursing home where they talked with our senior citizens, performed for them, and helped them with household chores.

Fourth, create a platform for students to show their talent. Display is an important part of habit-fostering. In light of openness and democratic participation, displaying platforms can be class-wide, grade-wide, or school-wide. Group activities featuring the demonstration and sharing of amicable habits not only help those with the habits further internalize them but also create an atmosphere for those without them to actively aspire for them. In Donghuan

Primary School of Jiaozuo, all school contests were organized around our monthly themes. Twelve contests focusing on 12 different themes held throughout the 12 months of a year provided the stage for all the students to show their best side and taught students the important lesson that competition was more about continually challenging and improving oneself than engaging in vicious competition against peers. Based on the experience learned from the previous year, the contests continued to evolve in form and style, always providing a fresh and challenging platform for all students.

Fifth, reflect, evaluate, and find beauty in diversity. Although reflection is directed inward and evaluation outward, both are important ways of finding our true self and internalizing truly good habits. Together, reflection and evaluation help complete the transition from practice to perseverance, from a newly acquired way of doing things to consciously and persistently internalized habits, and from forced obeying to willing compliance. We suggest that teachers and students all write down reflections of themselves and evaluation of others toward the end of every month. Reflection and evaluation can take different forms but should always stay close to the monthly theme. Many schools have taken the initiative to engage not only students, but also their parents and teachers in the "daily reflection, weekly evaluation, and monthly awarding" practice. It serves well in reminding students of the importance of abiding by rules anytime, anywhere. In Qiaoxi District of Shijiazhuang, schools launched a "Monthly Star" program. Students were awarded "star medals" for outstanding performance in specific areas based on their personal statement, class recommendations, and school evaluations. For example, a student might be rewarded for his or her contribution to environmental protection or volunteer service. Every school had a "Starlight Valley," where monthly exhibitions told the stories of our little craftsmen such as tree planters and rose growers.

iii. Operational Tips for Carrying Out the One Thing per Month Initiative

Experience shows that in order to make the One Thing per Month initiative work, we should not only attach importance to the fostering of habits, but also develop an effective working mechanism together with a set of operational methods. Here are some operational tips.

First, ensure the participation of all stakeholders and systematic designing. Despite its classroom-based nature, the One Thing per Month initiative will not produce the expected results unless schools render their support and all stakeholders are engaged. Therefore, it is very important to set up a working mechanism where the school principal takes charge and all stakeholders, including the moral education faculty and head teachers, take part. The head of a school should play a primary role in the moral education of students and the fostering of useful habits. The management of the initiative should benefit from the seamless integration and smooth coordination of principals, deputy principals, grade deans, head teachers, parents, and students. The school should take charge of developing yearly action plans and work programs. At the beginning (end) of every month, the school should issue the monthly plan of the present (coming) month to all teachers so that they can develop class action plans and teaching programs accordingly. The head teacher or the Perfect Classroom program team designs the specific process, making it operational and action-oriented while subject teachers integrate each monthly theme into their own subject. The nurturing of the humanistic spirit in the Chinese class, rational thinking in the mathematics class, and appreciation of artistic beauty in the music class, the physical education class, and the art class serves as good means to habit-fostering. Strengthening the connection between schools, families, and society, we will make better use of community-based educational resources to render the One Thing per Month initiative more open in form, richer in content, and more diverse and flexible in organization. The experience of various experimental zones and experimental schools shows that uniform planning at the school level better integrates resources than individual classroom actions and serves the purpose of creating an environment where all players learn from each other and grow hand in hand.

Second, identify priorities for spiral growth. Different from the traditional way of education that makes efforts in all aspects but works on no priorities, our One Thing per Month initiative accurately grasps the laws governing children's physical and mental growth and their needs for social interaction and adopts a habit-fostering approach featuring careful selection of activities, step-by-step implementation of plans, focused attention to priorities, and spiral growth for students. This approach divides a student's pre-college school life into kindergarten, primary school (lower grade, middle grade, and higher grade), junior high school, and senior high school. The ultimate goal is to help students acquire, sustain, and internalize the 12 primary habits and 36 second-layer habits.

In kindergarten (3- to 6-year-olds), we focus on habits related to taking care of oneself and initially befriending others. In primary school (6- to 12-year-olds), we stress reading, learning, social interaction, and self-improvement, but all at an elementary level. In junior high school (12- to 15-year-olds), we devote our attention to advanced learning and comprehensive social interaction. In senior high school (15- to 18-year-olds), our focus shifts to research-based learning, deep social interaction, and refined taste.

Take kindergarten for example. Once a reporter interviewed a Nobel laureate and asked him where he received the best education. The Nobel laureate said it was in kindergarten, because that was where he learned to play, to share, and to love. Of course, habits are not acquired overnight, and internalization can be long and painstaking. Children may acquire good habits in kindergarten but still need to work on them in primary school and high school.

Third, make explicit requirements and encourage innovation. For each month, we have laid out the theme, primary habit, and second-layer habits explicitly. Discretion comes in for model activities. Different requirements can be made for different age groups, resulting in different choices of the monthly thing. Take January as an example. In this month, we focus on thrift, and the overall goal is saving and being frugal. Second-layer habits include saving, being temperate, and being thrifty. In order to save, students may need to observe several rules while eating, such as only order what one can eat, never spill drinks, and pack up leftovers. In order to be temperate, students may need to refrain from excess in eating, drinking, spending money, playing, watching TV, and surfing the Internet. In order to be thrifty, students may need to cherish what they have and refrain from blindly following fashion and pursuing an extravagant lifestyle and famous brands. These are all the habits that a school needs to prioritize according to its specific conditions and the requirements of different classes before integrating them into action plans.

Despite its explicitly stated monthly themes and targeted habits, the One Thing per Month initiative never closes the door to innovative implementation. We insist on adhering to the core concept of new education and the basic requirements of excellent curriculum. We insist on aspiring to the 12 primary habits and the 36 second-layer habits. Most importantly, we insist on innovation and the adaptation to specific needs of different regions, schools, and age groups. Haimen Experimental Primary School has set a good example by launching a "Ten Skills" course. The ten skills include cleaning one's room, preparing five dishes, swimming, beautiful handwriting, playing a ball game, playing a musical instrument, editing a newsletter, giving a performance, hosting a meeting, and making small inventions. The first six skills are compulsory, while the last four are optional and can be replaced by other skills. In 2014, Haimen Experimental Primary School followed the instruction of the Civic Enhancement Office of Jiangsu Province and launched the "Eight Manners and Four Rituals" program. Students are taught manners in relation to their appearance, bearing, talking, interacting, walking, watching, visiting, and dining through four rituals, namely, the school entrance ceremony, growth ceremony, youth ceremony, and coming of age ceremony. This program covers almost all areas of a student's life and is highly practical and accessible.

Rather than limiting attention to one thing only every month, the One Thing per Month initiative approaches the 12 monthly themes throughout a year holistically and in that way establishes a complete educational ecosystem that conforms to children's life rhythm. The 12 primary habits run through the program and are substantiated by knowledge and skills. Together, they create a happy and all-around educational life. One Thing per Month connects the dots, links our paths, and leads students on the way toward a happy, complete, and inspired life.

III. Case Study: Promoting One Thing per Month Under the New Education Framework in the Primary School Affiliated to Haimen Experimental School of Jiangsu

Listed below are some of the unique features of One Thing per Month: it focuses on core competences and aims to foster habits that will benefit students for the rest of their life; it starts with small things but always works for improvement and enrichment; it materializes through concrete events such as reading, practicing, researching, and writing activities; it also teaches students how to listen, speak, and even use the Internet; and it combines civic education, life education, artistic education, and intellectual education.

The following is a case study of how One Thing per Month is planned and implemented in the Primary School Affiliated to Haimen Experimental School of Jiangsu.

Theme: Environmental Protection

January: "Protection in Action"

In January, we organized "Protection in Action" as our One Thing per Month.

On our beautiful campus, students were darting around like white pigeons and recording their daily life with cameras. They were our little health journalists who spread the message of environmental protection through the modeling behaviors of their schoolmates. "Send Garbage Home" was another program that attracted the participation of all students. With everyone paying attention, our classrooms and hallways became unprecedentedly clean and tidy. "Walk the Green Way Hand in Hand" witnessed the joint efforts of our students and their parents to build green parks and communities. In the "Environmental Fashion Show," students in lower grades made clothes with plastic bags, cartons, beverage bottles, and other recyclable materials. Students in higher grades drafted "Water Saving Proposals" and research reports on "How to Cut Paper in a More Saving Way." Environmental protection had turned from an idea to an action. Through these programs, we were not only planting a green seed in every young heart, but also preparing them for their future mission of making the earth a beautiful home.

Theme: Learning

February: The First Lesson in the Lunar New Year

In February, we organized "Lesson on Zodiac Animals" as our One Thing per Month.

Every school year began with the Lesson on Zodiac Animals. In order to celebrate the Year of Monkey in 2016, we integrated the image of a gold monkey into the winter vacation assignment book for every grade. The book covered all the subjects a student was studying. In order to finish all the assignments, students would need to work with their parents, carry out online researches, do extra reading, and even design mascots. The Lesson on Zodiac Animals was carefully designed to include six modules, namely, Singing a Song in the Year of Monkey, Making A Wild Guess, Recommending Your Mascot, Monkey Culture, Monkey Stories, and New Ambitions for the Year of Monkey. Students were naturally drawn to such cultural events on Zodiac Animals and would always find them an interesting and inspiring way to begin a new semester.

Theme: Charity

March: "A Journey of Love"

In March, our One Thing per Month focused on passing love to people in need.

In March 2014, we decided to launch our Sunshine Charity Program in Xihe Primary School of Xixiang County, Shaanxi Province, after a careful online survey. It was a village school built on the hillside in a poverty-stricken area. The total number of teachers and students combined was smaller than 100, of whom many were left-behind children. We signed a three-year cooperation agreement with the school and organized regular donations for it to build more reading rooms and buy more desks, dinner sets, and school uniforms. In 2014, we sent 11 teachers and students to Xihe Primary School. After that, it became a regular practice for us to send students there every year so that our students could better understand the life of their peers in the countryside. Last year, we invited teachers and students of Xihe Primary School to visit us. Together, we spent a wonderful week.

Shaanxi is the starting point. From there, we have embarked on a journey of love, bringing love to people around us and people far from us. A one-time action has become a long-term program.

Theme: Diligence

April: "Go to the Farm"

In April, "Go to the Farm" was our monthly event to promote diligence.

Last year, on a piece of land to the north of the school playground we built the Sunshine Farmland. It was where our course on farming was to be taught. The land was divided into 42 pieces with low brick walls, and each class was given one piece to farm. In the eyes of our children, these lands were their Funny Fish Pool, Moon River, and Dream Garden. In their spare time, students ploughed the soil, sowed seeds, and removed weeds under the guidance of their parents. Bustling with our children and full of energy and hope, Sunshine Farmland promised a good harvest and an experience of life on the farm.

More importantly, they would be able to taste the joy of harvest and feel more keenly the vigor of nature after a year of hard work.

Theme: Aesthetics

May: "My Stage, My Performance"

In May, we focused on aesthetics and launched the "My Stage, My Performance" event.

Our one-month campus art festival titled "Sunshine, Star, and Show" provided an opportunity for all students to show their talents. In their spare time, students devoted themselves to preparing for the 13 contests to be held during the festival, covering singing, playing the piano, dancing, calligraphy, sculpturing, twirling the hula hoop, solving a Rubik's cube, and so on. During the week in mid-May when the contests took place, our children went on stage, beaming with confidence and ready to show their talent.

The art festival significantly enriched our campus life. It created a stage broad enough for all students to show their talent and would continue to shape our students' aesthetic taste and attainment.

Theme: Thrift

June: "We Are Having a Food Street!"

In June, we opened a food street to advocate thrift and temperance.

The school bicycle shed was turned to temporary food booths. In an effort to get a booth, students tried their best to prepare food in the most innovative way. In an effort to attract more customers, students made beautiful posters, formed marketing teams, and learned marketing strategies.

On the food street, our little vendors laid out all kinds of foods and called out to attract our little customers, who with their pocket money in hand, looked, compared, and bargained. It was such a busy scene!

In this way, our children learned how to spend their pocket money purposefully and reaped the joy of working with others and making new friends.

Theme: Sports and Fitness

July: "Let's Exercise!"

In July, we organized the "Let's Exercise!" event and called for more students to do sports.

Swimming is good for students' health, and the hot month of July is a perfect time for swimming. We tried our best to ensure that every student had access to the school swimming pool and could enjoy the fun of swimming. More than a skill, swimming sometimes saves lives. That was why our plan was supported by all parents. After 20 days of training, students were able to get rid of their swimming ring and dart in the pool like a school of fish. Their performance was evaluated, and those who could swim were called "fish in the pool," those who took part in the swimming contest "carp in the river," and those who swam every week "dolphin in the sea."

In addition to swimming, the school encouraged students to take part in a variety of fitness programs such as table tennis, tennis, football, basketball, aerobics, martial arts, and so on. With a whole month devoted to fitness-related activities, students began to give more importance to fitness programs, and their sports skills and health conditions were significantly improved.

Theme: Reflection

August: "Reflection Makes Us Better"

As the old saying goes, "the most difficult thing is to know yourself." In August, we focused on self-reflection.

Students in lower grades read *Magic Guess: I Am the Little Manager of Time* with their parents and kept a diary of their daily life with words and drawings. This proved to be an effective way to help students plan their day properly and regularly.

Besides making daily plans and regularly reflecting on their life and study, students in middle and higher grades were required to take part in special programs. Take the "Face Your Challenge" program for example. Middle-grade students were each given RMB 30 as pocket money and told not to use it until one month later. Those who successfully faced the challenge and refrained from spending the money in advance were recognized as having self-discipline and capable of following plans. Students in higher grades were required to record positive models and negative examples in their life through words, cartoon images, and videos; reflect on themselves with "a critical eye"; and try to "bring the best of themselves."

Theme: Obey Rules

September: "Let's Obey Rules!"

The cooling breeze of September brought to campus fresh faces. They were the first-year students. At the welcome ceremony, we launched a variety of events to stress rule-abiding behavior.

As they sang songs, listened to stories, read picture books, played games, and participated in contests under the guidance of their teachers, our newcomers learned not only to line up and walk hand in hand on campus, listen attentively in class, and always keep themselves clean and tidy, but all the manners and rules they were supposed to observe while studying, playing, eating, and sleeping. When requirements were incorporated into these interesting programs in a most natural and specific way, students became eager to learn and follow.

Our teachers followed the rules governing the physical and mental growth of our first-year students and explained requirements to them in the most patient and vivid way. They refrained from using such harsh words as "don't" and "forbid" when making orders. For example, a teacher seeing a student talking to others in a queue would gently remind him to "turn off the little trumpet." Another teacher telling students to sit still in class would say, "I am the commander of my body and I can control my hands and feet. Which commander cannot control his or her hands and feet?" These childlike talks enlivened training activities, and students often took the advice with a ready smile.

In this month, teachers worked together and taught by both words and acts. Hand in hand, they led first-year students into their classroom and helped them embrace campus life. Students learned to raise their hand to answer questions, listen attentively in class, and do homework carefully. They became accustomed to observing table manners, lining up, and walking on the right side of a road.

Although first-year students were our priority this month, we never forget students in other grades. They were required to review the songs of rules, work on weak points, help each other to make progress together, and even stage sitcoms on rule-abiding behavior. Students were invited to design their class growth book, on which they would record their growth path and keep track of all the gains and losses. *The Code of Conduct for Primary School Students* and the *Daily Behavior Norms for Primary School Students* were our guidelines when we set self-management and evaluation goals for students by grade. First- and second-grade students competed in mountain-climbing, running, and other similar sports games, while students in middle and higher grades participated in a wider range of point-winning activities. Their performance was reflected in their class show board. At the end of the month, the school selected students who best observed rules and had the best manners, and they became the role model for others.

These interesting and informative activities contributed to the beaming confidence and positive energy in our children and the good habits that were to benefit the rest of their life.

Theme: Confidence

October: "Confidence Shines"

In October, our school organized a rich variety of events to celebrate the monthly theme of "Confidence Shines." In each grade, students representing their classes were asked to introduce their favorite book to the audience. Our little scholars spoke with confidence and clarity and the winners proceeded to the school finals, where they were greeted with questions from their teachers. Once again, confidence shone through our contestants' calm and eloquent answers. "Sunshine Forum" provided another platform for all students to speak in front of their classmates on stage. Well prepared and all smiling, students shared their stories and won the applause of their peers. On Mondays and Fridays, we held the "Sunshine School Forum" during the lunch break. Outstanding class representatives were invited to speak in front of the whole school. The lecture hall on the second floor was always crowded during these days, with eloquent speakers and attentive listeners. It was a platform created by our school but enlivened by our children. It witnessed their shining moments as well as their growth path.

Theme: Gratitude

November: "Growth Ceremony"

In November, we organized a grand growth ceremony for students turning ten, where a tree of life was planted jointly by teachers and students. The month began with a number of themed activities. Students were invited to read books, find old photos, and tell growth stories to better understand "where I am from," sow seeds and watch the growth of plants, write letters to their parents to express their gratitude, learn to perform the Song of Gratitude by signs and sing the Happy Birthday song in English, participate in such games as "Protect the Egg" and "Home Alone," and write down their wishes on the "Dream Home" board in their classroom. The grand growth ceremony was held in the school stadium, and it told the story of our students' growth through four chapters. The important moment was witnessed by our students, their parents, and teachers.

Through these events, the children learned to be grateful, better understood the meaning of responsibility, and felt keenly the joy of loving others and being loved by others.

Theme: Friendliness

December: "Visit the Firefighter Training Camp"

In December, we organized a visit to the Firefighter Training Camp to help students become friendlier with others.

Haimen Fire Brigade was next to our school, which made it easier for us to develop this program. We held a grand opening ceremony to announce the establishment of Haimen Sunshine Youth Firefighter Academy, compiled a textbook for student firefighters, and offered courses on fire-fighting knowledge and drills. We created opportunities for our students to communicate with and learn from firefighters on campus, in the fire brigade, and in the community. This monthly themed event not only raised students' awareness of fire safety, but also helped them understand that effective cooperation came from friendly communication and mutual support between partners.

The One Thing per Month initiative allowed us to turn abstract principles into concrete actions and create for students an environment full of positive influence. From small things, our students acquired useful habits and learned how to behave themselves.

Five principles were observed as we implemented the One Thing per Month initiative.

1. Holistic approach

   In moral education, "5 + 2 = 0" is a thought-provoking metaphor that suggests five days of positive education at school can be offset by two days of negative influence at home. Fostering habits is a systematic project that requires a holistic approach. As one of the ten actions of new education, family–school cooperation naturally plays a part. Without the support of family members and educational resources in society, it is difficult for students to acquire and internalize good habits.

2. Self-motivation

   Fostering good habits requires the guidance of educators, the positive influence of the external environment, and the active efforts of individual students. Too much stress on external factors will only make matters worse. Therefore, new education chooses to focus on self-motivation and initiative, making the fostering of useful habits an active choice of students.

3. Practice

   The fostering of habits is essentially an organized educational activity. "What's learned from books is superficial after all; it's crucial to have it personally tested somehow." Habits are not taught but acquired in practice. Only through personal experience can students actively acquire and firmly internalize habits.

4. Life-oriented positioning

   Habits must come from real life. Social interactions provide the best scenario to test and evaluate their stability and appropriateness.

5. Integration

   The organic integration of education is reflected in the close connection between the fostering of habits and the teaching of subject matters.

In short, new education aspires to foster habits through a holistic, self-motivated, practice-centered, life-oriented, and integrated approach.

We believe that perfect planning is the premise, but concrete action is the key to ensure the effect of the One Thing per Month initiative. Therefore, it is to action that we devote the greatest attention, energy, and efforts. The way of action generally includes influencing (through environment), immersing (through reading), transforming (through classroom activities), experiencing (through practice), writing (sincere and wholeheartedly), expressing (through art), and internalization (through assessment).

Although teachers play the most important and direct role in helping students foster useful habits through the One Thing per Month initiative, we should always remember that the school is only one of the many players. Teachers should never exaggerate their own role but readily recognize the contribution of other educational factors, especially the obvious influence of parents on their children.

Exam scores are important, especially those of the National College Entrance Examination. However, scores only matter for the time being. Students who are admitted to famous colleges with high scores may not be able to live a successful life if they fail to develop the useful habits and core competencies central to their success. "What can our children rely on to live a full life?" In fact, the influence of education is limited. Only habits can accompany a person through the long journey of life.

That is why we say, "One thing per month, one habit for life."

The above case from pages 130–137 is provided by Bian Huishi, School Principal of Haimen Experiment Zone of Jiangsu Province.

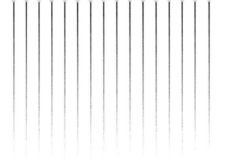

10

The New Education Experiment and Home–School Cooperation

I. The New Education Experiment's Propositions on Family Education
II. Practice of Home–School Cooperation in the New Education Experiment
III. Case Studies

Parents are the first teachers and family the permanent school of a child.

The New Education Experiment argues that without the development of parents, students' development won't be possible. The future social progress depends on the spirit of the next generation, which is shaped by education. Of the education one receives throughout a lifetime, family education is a vital part and has a fundamental, lifelong impact on one's personal growth. Therefore, it is naturally a key mission of the New Education Experiment to improve family education and promote home–school cooperation.

I. The New Education Experiment's Propositions on Family Education

The New Education Experiment's propositions on family education are mainly from the perspectives of parents, children, and families as a whole. This is manifested in the following ways.

i. Parents Are the First Teachers of a Child

Parents are the first people a child encounters in the world and the first teachers, with lifelong impact on the child. French educator F. Froebel once said, "The hand that rocks the cradle is the hand that rules the world." Liang Qichao also observed, "There two essentials for ruling the world: moral cultivation and talent cultivation. Both of them must start from childhood education which starts with family education. Therefore women's education is essential for a country's future." Our society has stressed school education so much that many parents are not aware that family education is the basis and key to a child's future. They are not aware that child education is the most challenging and complicated task in their adulthood and the most important task for human society.

Many believe that parenting is about feeding and clothing and leave education entirely to schools. In reality, no matter where the child is, he is always under the shadow of family education, shaped by the manners and words of his parents. A child without family education might go bad, and a child wrongly educated by parents might become worse. Generally speaking, a great child tends to have a loving family, and a child with character flaws often comes from a family of conflicts and tension.

Most parents haven't received any scientific training on child raising and tend to make mistakes. A good parent should not view child education as a boring obligation, but a fun and spiritual fulfilment. Only when parents take pleasure from education can they do the parenting job well.

ii. Childhood Is the Most Critical Period in One's Life
One's personality, thinking, and language competency start to take shape before and in the early stage of schooling. As Suhomlinski pointed out in the *Education Trilogy*, "Childhood is the most important period of one's life. It is the preparation for the future, but is itself a true, splendid, unique, and unrepeatable life. Therefore, what kind of adult a child will grow into depends on how and with whom his childhood is spent and what he has learned and taken in from his surroundings in his childhood."

Family education is of particular importance for a child under age five. Tolstoy once said, "What a child takes from the surroundings for intellect, emotions, will and character from his birth to his turning five is times more than what he takes from age five to his deathbed."

iii. Family Education Is the Weakest Link
English scholar Thomas Henry Huxley once said, "A great nation must be built upon family education." But in China, the value of family education is underestimated.

Maria Montessori once warned us: mistreating children is more disastrous than mistreating adults. Inappropriately treated, a child might avenge the society after growing up. Mistreatment will hinder the personality development of a child who is weak, passive, and vulnerable—in comparison, an adult will be aware of such mistreatment and can choose to fight back. Therefore, mistreating children will cause more horrific consequences than mistreating adults.

Unlike driving, which requires a driver's license beforehand, parenting requires no prior training or certification. As a result, there are many "unlicensed" parents. In fact, parenting is far more complicated and difficult than driving. Good parenting requires knowledge about nearly everything of a child, from his physical and psychological status, how he should be raised, his academic studies, the cultivation of his personality, and so on. But in reality, you need no prior training in these aspects to be a parent, to order your child around. We don't know how many parents out there have no common sense of parenting or education and are unqualified for parenting, but we know they are very common. A road full of "unlicensed drivers" must be dangerous to travel.

iv. Home–School Cooperation Is the Most Effective Way of Education

Home–school cooperation may take the form of home–school interaction, the parent–child reading program, the new parent school, and the home–school cooperation committee. We should strengthen the home–school cooperation mechanism, introduce new means of home–school cooperation, engage parents more in school life, and guide parents to grow with their children, so that family education and school education can reinforce and complement each other and achieve coordinated development.

Home–school cooperation will help bring out the educational function of family; establish the modern school system; improve educational quality, the degree of satisfaction with school education, the teacher–student relationship, and the family relationship; and allow parents and children to make progress together.

The parent committee is a key part of the modern school system that is law-abiding and autonomous with public supervision and engagement. It is an effective way to give parents an active role in educational reform and to construct a collaboration system among schools, families, and society.

Many examples have shown us the tremendous benefits parents can bring to school administration. Home–school cooperation has transformed negative interference of parents into positive engagement and contribution and changed the school environment.

II. Practice of Home–School Cooperation in the New Education Experiment

Shortly after the New Education Experiment was launched, we set up a research group dedicated to the improvement of home–school cooperation and even introduced home–school cooperation as the seventh major action of the experiment. We co-initiated the New Parent School with *Mochou* magazine in Jiangsu. The school is set up to advance the New Education Experiment on all fronts by integrating educational resources, grow into a high-quality, high-level school of distinct characteristics of new education as soon as possible, promote the cooperation and common progress of family education and school education, offer comprehensive training to parents, help foster learning-oriented families and communities, and create a favorable environment for the all-around harmonious and healthy development of teenagers. By so doing, it aims to live up to the magazine's mission statement for spreading new ideas and improving the quality of family education; achieve the experiment's educational goal of "challenging oneself and chasing ideals"; promote people-centered, scientific, harmonious, and sustainable development; and help create an education-oriented and harmonious society.

The New Parent School upholds that the school should be a place where students and teachers make progress together. Home and the school are the two most important places for minors, so parents and teachers are coworkers and share the responsibilities for the intellectual development, personality cultivation, emotional maturity, strengthening of will, formation of values, outlook on the world and life, and so on. Compared to teachers, parents need more training on family education and on the physical and psychological development of children so that they can better understand and communicate with their children and communicate and work with teachers.

The New Parent School leadership consists of one principal who is generally concurrently the principal of New Education Experimental School, responsible for overall school administration; one assistant principal, who is responsible for external contacts, coordination, communication, inspection, and evaluation affairs; and several honorary principals and advisors who might be competent government officials, experts in home education, celebrities, or parents. It also has a home–school cooperation committee, which is comprised of representative parents, each representing one class. The committee members could be volunteers or recommended by the class headmaster in question and confirmed by the principal. The term of committee membership is renewable but will automatically expire once the member's child graduates from the school. The committee takes orders from the school leadership and contributes to the school's daily work. When conditions permit, the school can give the committee a bigger role in democratic and autonomous administration of the school.

The New Parent School was a key part of the New Education Experiment. It prepared the parent training plan and program every school year, and saw to it that the teachers, money, textbooks, and relevant readings needed were in place.

It held a plenary meeting at least once per semester, with regular meetings at the class and grade levels, to enhance communication and mutual understanding between teachers, parents, and students. It fully respected the opinions of parents and actively solicited their trust and support.

It organized regular parent training activities, including lectures and in-person information services, to effectively instill advanced ideas and methods on family education among the parents. Through training, the parents were expected to realize that parenting is a matter of national interests, take the initiative to fulfill parenting duties, value the moral education of children, teach children to follow social ethics and conventions, enhance their law awareness and sense of social responsibility, follow their children's progress in intellectual development and academic studies, and help them foster a good learning habit with reasonable requirements and in a scientific way. Parents should also help children develop a healthy lifestyle, encouraging them to take part in cultural, entertaining, and sports activities and social networking activities and promote their physical and mental development; guide children to share domestic chores within their capabilities; support them to contribute to public-interest activities; and teach them the skills to take care of themselves.

The New Parent School hosted regular parent–child activities such as exchange, dialogues, entertainment, study tours, and tourism; recommended books and magazines on family education to parents; organized the reading club, composition, speech contests, seminars, and parties; and advocates that parents should learn and grow together with their children. Based on the training effect, the practice of family education, and the progress of children, it selected and rewarded model parents and families once per school year with physical and spiritual awards, and actively took part in government-organized evaluations of family education at various levels.

All its activities were funded by the school budget and public donations. With the approval of the parent–school cooperation committee, it could charge parents for relevant fees and the money collected would be earmarked for the designated purpose, with the expenditure details released on a regular basis. The parent–school cooperation committee should actively play its role in coordination and communication to boost the school's autonomous administration and development.

It's a regret that the New Parent School has ceased to function due to the job shift of its leader, but it has successfully instilled the idea that "new education needs new parents" among all the new education practitioners.

In November 2011, Tong Xixi, a children's literature writer, initiated the public-interest program named the New Education Firefly Parent–Child Reading Program, on top of which the Parent–Child Reading Research Center was founded, later renamed New Parents Institute. Since then, the reading experience with children has been considered a key part of the development of new parents. In the past five years, the Morning Reading of New Parents column has attracted 200 million views in total, and the Firefly Parent–Child Reading Working Stations in over 40 Chinese cities have launched over 5,000 online and offline public-interest activities. In 2015, the New Education Academy co-launched the New Family Education Academy with Qtone Education Group, with Tong Xixi as the general director and child educator Mr. Sun Yunxiao as the president. The New Family Education Academy has compiled and published books such as the *Blue Book on Family Education in China* and *Book Series on Family Education in China*, conducted surveys on family education, and co-hosted the International Forum on Family Education with the Professional Committee on Family Education of the Chinese Society of Education, achieving desired effects.

III. Case Studies
i. Case 1: Home–School Cooperation Promoted in Haimen, Jiangsu Province

In September 2005, Haimen signed up for the New Education Experiment as a whole. Since then, this county-level city has built up its reputation across Jiangsu and even China on its promotion of new education, in which family education plays a vital part.

a. The Family Education Day

Haimen launched its first Family Education Day on January 6, 2007, under the theme of "building a harmonious society and growing together with children," to advocate that "parents and children should live and create a beautiful life together." A total of 25 kindergartens and primary and middle schools across the city became New Parents Schools. The event gathered a number of famous experts and scholars active in family education and attracted nearly 10,000 parents in the audience.

The second Family Education Day was celebrated on January 5, 2008, under the theme of "teaching children good habits that will benefit them for the rest of their life." The composition contest and the home visit day activity were organized across the city to warm up the atmosphere. On the Family Education Day, a salon on the cultivation of good habits was organized in primary and middle schools across the city, with parents invited to exchange with each other and teachers on how to help children foster good habits. As a result, the mutual understanding and consensus between parents and schools were enhanced.

On January 3, 2009, the third Family Education Day celebrated the theme of "reading together, growing together." Haimen organized a voting campaign for reading families and selected 100 model reading families with children in primary and middle schools, calling for creating a harmonious environment for parent–child reading. Peng Yi, an expert in child education, gave a lecture entitled "Illustrated Books—The Seed of Happiness" to parents of kindergarten children, and Nanjing University set up a family education advisory team to give tour lectures in primary and middle schools across the city.

On January 9, 2010, the fourth Family Education Day was marked under the theme of "learning to learn and grow together." Haimen acknowledged 100 model parents and organized a competition on theses on family education. Vice President Sun Yunxiao of the China Youth & Children Research Association and President Yin Jianqin of the Institute of Early Childhood Education of Jiangsu Academy of Educational Sciences each gave a lecture.

On January 8, 2011, the fifth Family Education Day was marked under the theme of "growing together," calling for parents to read, play sports, work, perform, and engage in DIY activities with their children to create a wonderful life together. A city-wide family talent TV contest was hosted.

On January 7, 2012, the sixth Family Education Day was marked under the theme of "playing together." On that day, schools across the city organized colorful parent–child games, which brought the parents and children closer to each other, and gave them a happy, relaxing day.

On January 22, 2013, the seventh Family Education Day was marked under the theme of "caring for children's mental health." The attention was directed to the mental health of the children. The feature entitled Maintaining the Mental Health of Minors was produced and screened for nearly 10,000 parents, and volunteers offering psychological consultation to children were awarded, calling for the society to pay attention to and contribute to the mental health of the children.

In 2014, the eighth Family Education Day was extended to a family education week lasting from January 4 to 11, under the theme of "social etiquette." A promotional video on social etiquette was screened for the parents. At the Desheng Primary School, students performed an etiquette demonstration on campus. Deputy Secretary General Ms. Cao Ping and Chen Yiyun of the China Youth & Children Research Association each gave a lecture for 5,000 parents in Haimen.

On January 16, 2015, the ninth Family Education Day was marked under the theme of "family education on etiquette." Nine salons of family education on etiquette were organized by parent volunteers to share stories and experience in teaching children social etiquette at home, so as to create a favorable environment for promoting etiquette education at home.

On January 12, 2016, the tenth Family Education Day was marked under the theme of "I love my home." Representatives of teachers and parents were invited to the exhibition of achievements of the past ten editions of Family Education Day, and they were all awed by the miracle of time and persistence.

In the past decade, to mark the annual Family Education Day, major activities were organized at the city level, in addition to activities of distinct characteristics at the school level. It is a one-day event with influence felt throughout the year, promoting family education in the city in a progressive way. It has attracted the participation of over 30 experts in family education, inspection visits by over 20 teams from inside and outside Jiangsu, and the coverage of over 30 mainstream media including Xinhua News Agency and *China Youth Daily*, generating a huge social impact. Haimen has been recognized as a national model city in family education. Shang Xiuyun, an expert in family education, once proposed to the National Political Consultative Conference to establish the National Family Education Day, following the footprints of Haimen.

The Family Education Day is an innovation of the New Education Experiment. It boosts and guides family education with the philosophy of school education and forms benign interaction between family education and school education. Meanwhile, the authoritative and influential experts in family education invited to the event have pointed out the direction for parents. More importantly, it has grown beyond a festival into the beacon lighting up the bittersweet and fruitful journey of parenting and family education.

b. The New Parents School: The Class on Family
Education and Parenting
The class is generally for students, but in Haimen, there is a special class for parents, known as the New Parents School, which can be found in every school in the city and has become a solid front for promoting family education. Each school will organize regular training activities of various kinds to help parents command scientific ways of child education and work with schools in educating the children. Now there are over 80 model parents schools in Haimen and 16 model parents schools in Nantong.

Dongzhou Middle School in Haimen has registered the Family Education Guidance Center, which is dedicated to family education services and offers not-for-profit family education guidance, training, exchange, and consultation services. The center hires 18 experts in family education to organize two training and guidance sessions every semester and offer free consultation and guidance on family education every week to parents in need. It not only introduces scientific, reasonable family education methods to parents, but also continues to engage in sustainable practice and scientific, up-to-date, and reasonable research on family education, so as to promote students' development through family education. It is thus nicknamed by parents as the "parenting advancement camp."

Zhengda Primary School is the smallest school in Haimen. It regularly awards model parents and shares their family education stories and experience on the publicity board on campus to other parents.

Just as children have their own doubts about growing up, parents have their confusion about family education. Each family is different from the others and has its own conflicts and confusion. There is no one-size-fits-all solution for them. But each family can receive pertinent consultation and aide from the New Parents School. Here they can draw inspiration from other parents' success and receive professional guidance and consultation. The New Parents School is open to every parent and every family.

c. Parent Volunteers

Via the home–school cooperation committee, Haimen continues to enhance home–school communication and cooperation, and stimulate parents' enthusiasm in engaging in school administration and interacting with the school to produce the synergy effect. To engage more parents in school administration, schools across the city have set up their own parent volunteer team to maximize parents' role in school education.

For example, Dongzhou Primary School introduced courses given by volunteer parents on top of the home–school cooperation committee.

At the reading class every Friday, moms, dads, or even grandparents are invited to tell a story to the class. The home–school cooperation committee would also invite parents to the campus to introduce their line of work to the students. For instance, a mother who is a doctor can teach students knowledge about teeth, a dad who is a police officer can share stories about heroes, and a parent who is a bookstore owner can introduce different kinds of books to the students.

The school and the home–school cooperation committee have co-designed 100 tour programs for the students, such as "Know Your Hometown" and "Visiting Tourist Attractions on the Textbook." Parent volunteers are recruited for each class, and more and more parents are encouraged to take part in these tour programs.

The school has also launched the digital community course in which parents and children would develop and maintain the blog, QQ group, and WeChat group of the class together. In the digital community, volunteer parents will gather and discuss problems and issues troubling the children and then have heart-to-heart conversations with them to clear their doubts and offer psychological help. The school will also organize regular online salons on family education to share parent's experience in family education and promote common progress.

For another example, Dongzhou Kindergarten of Haimen has set up the Parent Volunteers Association with the coordination of the home–school cooperation committee. The Parent Volunteers Association has a standing committee composed of members of the home–school cooperation committee and the school leadership. The standing committee will see to it that parent volunteers will do at least one thing for the children in the kindergarten every school year, such as organizing outings and spring tours and providing security services.

The kindergarten faces a busy road leading to the central market, with heavy traffic of pedestrians and vehicles. Traffic jams are common at the intersection during rush hours. To address the problem, parent volunteers are organized to police the traffic. Every morning, they wait in front of the kindergarten and open the door when a car stops to drop off the child, so that the driving parent won't need to get out the car to see the child off and can leave immediately for work. After school, they would guide parents to park their car in good order and take their child to the car. In this way, the traffic conditions in front of the kindergarten have been much improved. In the past years, parent volunteers have been growing in numbers and play a key role in ensuring the children's security in addition to the school and parents. The municipal education bureau has called on all kindergartens to establish their own parent volunteer association.

The Primary School Affiliated to Haimen Experimental Middle School has formed a home–school cooperation committee by grade and opens its door to parents who are honest, upright, interested, loving, resourceful, capable, and have spare time, instead of those in power and of high social status. Parents meeting the above requirements are encouraged to volunteer, and the final list is determined by the school leadership. The home–school cooperation committee is also asked to spot and tap the artistic talents of parents of each grade, organize colorful activities for student clubs, and promote the healthy development of students. With the help of parents, the school has opened student clubs on flower arrangement, baking, DIY, magic, and so on. Last year, it even cleared a lot to teach students how to plant. Volunteer parents teach the fourth-graders how to bake delicious, additive-free cookies to improve their hands-on ability and add flavor to ordinary life. Parents have made up for the shortage of teachers and helped cultivate students' talents, and their courses have been warmly welcomed by students and other parents alike.

Parents are a valuable asset of education. They can make up for the weakness of school education and complement school teaching. By engaging in school education via various means, parents will have a better understanding of school administration and school life, observe and experience the school life from a new perspective, and gradually see school affairs and class affairs as their own business. Parents can contribute their wisdom and time to school development, and make up for and improve school education. This can be seen as an extended part of school administration.

d. Parent–Child Activities: A Mind Bridge

Parent–child reading has become a trend. It is aimed to teach children how to read, the most important learning skill in one's life, in the most loving, natural way. Children and adults are generally living in two worlds, but by reading the same book, their worlds are bridged and they will have a "common language and code." The experience is very important for both children and adults. Therefore, in past years, Haimen has launched various kinds of parent–child reading contests and voting campaigns for reading families to advocate parent–child reading.

At the end of every semester, each class in Haimen will stage a celebration for students to show their progress made in the past semester to their parents; remind students, teachers, and parents of all the great moments of the semester; create a happy memory; and further bond school education with family education.

The first day in kindergarten, the moment when the red scarf was tied, the year the child turned 10, and the year the child turned 18—it is of special meaning to mark these big moments of a child's life. To this end, each primary school in Haimen will stage a ceremony for the 10-year-olds, each junior middle school a youth ceremony, and each high school the coming-of-age celebration, leaving unforgettable memories in the hearts of parents and students.

Head of the municipal education bureau, Xu Xinhai once said, "Our schools aim to be a paradise not just for teachers and students, but also parents, allowing parents to grow once again with their children." We believe that home–school cooperation will have an even brighter future in Haimen.

ii. Case 2: Home–School Cooperation in Tianyi No. 3 Experimental Primary School in Ningcheng County, Chifeng City, Inner Mongolia

Originally named Tianbei Primary School, Tianyi No. 3 Experimental Primary School is a remote rural school in the county seat of Ningcheng of Chifeng City, a thousand-year-old city with picturesque scenery. It joined the New Education Experiment in 2011, and in just a few years it has grown from a village school with 1,400 students to a county-level school with 2,743 students in 44 classes and 149 teachers and staffers.

In the past years, it has been exploring an effective path of home–school education with agreement in action and faith, and offered a wonderful stage for the healthy growth of students.

a. Inviting Parents to the Class

In September 2011, the tiered reading course featuring "reading in the morning and at noon and reflecting in the evening" was introduced to the school. A number of books recommended by the New Education Experiment were

---

The above case 1 from pages 144–149 is contributed by Chen Xinting from Haimen Muninicipal Education Bureau in Jiangsu Province.

purchased for the students. While teachers and students were absorbed in the pleasure of reading, many parents were worried that reading extracurricular books was a waste of time and might affect the children's academic performance, so they banned such books at home, which really upset the students. So how to show the parents the beauty of this course?

In November that year, the school invited representative parents to a demonstration class on morning and noon reading. In the morning reading session in Class 3 of Grade 5, teacher Zhu Hongyan read out the poem "I Am a Little Butterfly" as a birthday gift to student Ren Xiaomeng and asked Ren's father to come to the front of the class. The father and the other parents present were moved to tears by the emotional reading and the wonderful moment the students were creating. In Class 2 of Grade 4, parents were invited to a lecture given by teacher Chen Likun on the story "The Hundred Dresses." They were impressed by the story's effect on the students and realized that the story of its heroine, Wanda, spoke louder than their dry sermons in daily life. After the lecture, they rushed to share their feelings and what they had learned. The school then took the chance to bring home to the parents the importance of reading and writing skills, and the value of extracurricular books, and encourage them to read together with their children. Some well-educated parents have responded positively to the call.

To give parents a better understanding of what school education was about and what we were doing, and to track the development of teachers and students, in March 2012, the school initiated a thread entitled "Seeds of Dandelion" on the Education Online website, in addition to dozens of other threads posting teachers' essays on education. The 40 classes in the school also launched their respective thread to track the colorful school life of students and the development of teachers and parents. Parents were shown how to log on and use the website so that they could play a role in school life and grow together with students and teachers. In this way, parents could also make their voice heard, make suggestions, and reach consensus with the school. This website has thus gradually grown into a digital community of the school and a spiritual home for its teachers, students, and parents.

b. Co-creating a Poetic Educational Life with Parents

In August 2013, Tong Xixi, president of the New Parents Institute, was invited to give a lecture on parent–child reading to teachers, students, and parents. By sharing his reading experience, Mr. Tong, a noted children's literature writer, kindled the interest in reading among parents and children. From then on, parents started to volunteer to buy books and read books with their children. Zihan's mother has been buying books for the class since then. Yuanyuan's father has been reading with Yuanyuan since then—they spend at least one hour per day reading children's books such as *La Petite Poule qui voulait voir la Mer* by Christian Jolibois, *Xiaogui Xidangjia* by Tong Xixi, and *J. H. Fabre's Book of*

Insects. The reading hour has become the happiest family time of the day. Day by day, Yuanyuan's demeanor and speech have improved significantly, which inspires other parents to follow their lead and read with their own children. More and more families have started to embrace the joy of reading. The parent–child reading experience has become a trend across the campus.

The listening-reading-drawing-speech course is a highlight of the new education curriculum, a magic wand to enlighten the children upon the joy of reading and writing. To encourage parents of the first- and second-graders to read and write with their children, teachers would display the works by students online, communicate with parents, and award parents who have done a good job in writing with their children. The first-graders don't know how to write yet, so they would draw first, and then explain their drawing to their parents who would write it down to complete the drawing-writing assignment. Many children who have underachieved in exams have surprised their parents with their amazing creativity and imagination shown in the listening-reading-drawing-speech course. When parents start to believe that their children are the best, both parents and children will make remarkable progress in no time. At the second-grade level, teachers ask parents to add a few words to every drawing-writing assignment, which parents gladly do. In this way, the listening-reading-drawing-speech course creates a platform for children, parents, and teachers to have heart-to-heart conversations and grow together.

For the medium- and advanced-grades, the school offers a special practice course on traditional Chinese festivals and the 24 solar terms. Under the guidance of teachers, the students are asked to determine their own topic, read extensively on it, design a tour program according to the characteristics of the festival or folk custom they chose, and make the tour together with their parents. Besides offering company, parents should guide and "fund" the tour within their capabilities, such as accompanying the children to a Spring Festival fair, to the field, or to visit relatives and friends. Returning home, children will then write the experience down in their travel notes. In this way, parents and children together perform the miracle of "reading, writing, and living together."

Thanks to the family–school cooperation and the deep involvement of parents, we have created a miracle of educational life and new education through the initiative of "reading in the morning and noon and reflecting in the evening" and "reading, writing, and living together."

c. Introducing Public-Interest Parent–Child Reading Programs
To offer systematic guidance on parent–child reading and family education, in September 2013, the school introduced the Firefly Parent–Child Reading program, and opened a QQ group entitled The Firefly Light of New Education, through which the principal would forward the daily morning and evening articles and the Wednesday lectures from the New Education Firefly

headquarters to the parents to help them foster the reading habit and change their life through reading.

On October 21, 2014, Tong Xixi, the initiator of the "New Children" rural reading project, was invited to the school to give a two-hour lecture to over 4,700 teachers, students, and parents. The parents were moved by Ms. Tong's devotion to philanthropy and amazed by her superb oral composition skills. Since then, parent–child reading and oral composition have become part of students' daily life and a highlight of our school life. Parents are often proud to share their reading experience on the QQ group of the class.

Along with the "New Children" rural reading project came 100,000 yuan-worth children's books donated from Nanchang. Teachers and parents volunteered to work overtime to catalogue and shelve these books for the students as soon as possible. A volunteer mother shared with great pride how she read with her child and how much her child loved reading while sorting out the books.

On the last day of the semester, parents and children lined up early in front of the reading room, waiting to borrow books for the winter vocation. Ten days ago, the school distributed the Proposal for Parent–Child Reading to parents and posted a thread themed on parent–child reading in the winter vocation on the Education Online website. Parents and students would post their reading experience on the website, and teachers would read and leave comments to take the reading experience a step further.

When the spring semester began, some classes voted to have their model families promote the sustainable development of the parent–child reading project. Now, the love for reading is no longer exclusive to students and teachers but is shared by parents, too. Besides broadening the mind, the reading experience has cemented the partnership between teachers and parents and truly brought school education and family education together.

On January 21, 2014, the Firefly Light of New Education was officially renamed Ningcheng Branch of the Firefly Project, extending from parents of the No. 3 Experimental Primary School to all parents in Ningcheng County and even in Chifeng, in an attempt to engage more parents and families in reading. This has motivated our volunteer teachers and parents to work harder to deliver high-quality outcomes. For example, our volunteer parents have started to plan their own reading projects, starting with books such as *Dear Andrew, Raising Good Kids through Reading*, and *A Good Mother Is Better than a Good Teacher*.

The school has founded the Firefly Reading Club and the Firefly Family Reading Club to guide more parents to make better use of the donated books. Parents not only offer material and financial support for activities of the reading clubs, but also elevate the clubs' level with their own reading achievements.

The above case 2 from pages 149–152 is contributed by Li Xiuyun, deputy party secretary of Tianyi No. 3 Experimental Primary School of Ningcheng County, Chifeng City, Inner Mongolia, head of the Ningcheng Branch of New Education Firefly Program.

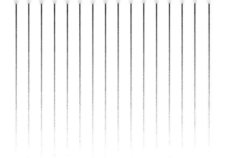

11

The New Education Experiment and Regional Education Development

The New Education Experiment is a nongovernmental reform and exploration in the education sector, free of administrative interference. It is built on participants' common ideals, pursuit, faith, and bond. Once you join the new education community, you need to obey its code of conduct. Therefore, it is an important mission for the new education community to determine how to implement the ideas, projects, and courses of the New Education Experiment, how to administer experimental areas, and how to bring new education to a higher level.

I. The Birth and Development of New Education Experimental Areas

The first new education experimental school was launched in Kunshan, Jiangsu Province, in 2002. Since then, the New Education Experiment has been gaining popularity with its ideas and actions and attracted more and more schools. In 2004, local governments in Jiangyan of Jiangsu Province and Qiaoxi District in Shijiazhuang of Hebei Province were the first in the country to promote local schools within their respective jurisdiction to join the experiment. In 2006, the first working meeting for new education experimental areas was convened in Xiuzhou District, Jiaxing, Zhejiang Province. At the meeting, I delivered a report entitled "Ten Keywords for New Education Experimental Zones," listing the following ten major issues for administering new education experimental areas: leadership, organizational structure, backbone force, experimental plan, activity implementation, funding, experience exchange, publicity, presentation, and evaluation. By 2006, there were 503 new education experimental schools across the country, 359 of which were from experimental areas, outnumbering those from nonexperimental areas. From then on, developing and administering experimental areas was considered the main way to promote the experiment, and working meetings of experimental areas were held in Xiaoshan of Zhejiang, Jiangxian of Shanxi, Jiaozuo of Henan, Huoqiu of Anhui, Qingyang of Gansu, Kuitun of Xinjiang, and Suixian of Hubei successively to discuss the practice and exploration of experimental areas. By June 2016, there were nine municipal-level experimental areas, 111 county-level experimental areas, 2,928 experimental schools, and over 3.2 million teachers and students contributing to the experiment across the country.

At the 2009 working meeting of experimental areas held in Jiangxian, we made it clear that the first and the most important thing in promoting the New Education Experiment on the regional scale was to reconstruct the local daily educational life with the ideas and actions of new education. The New Education Experiment should not be separated from the daily educational life but should be part of it and integrated into the curriculum. The effect of the experiment depends on whether it has become an indispensable part of local education, whether it is deeply rooted among the teachers, and whether it has been materialized in the real educational life, in the curriculum, and in the everyday life of teachers and students. In particular, incorporating the actions and ideas of new education into the curriculum is the key to the development of experimental areas. New education won't survive outside the curriculum. So far, the "morning and noon reading and evening reflection," the life education course, the ideal classroom, the ideal class, the one-thing-per-month initiative, and family–school cooperation advocated by the New Education Experiment have become part of the daily educational life in many experimental areas.

Meanwhile, we have raised some requirements for the development of experimental areas, such as following the experimental procedures, using standard terminology of new education, accumulating experimental materials, following the updates on the New Education Experiment, and adopting the "bottom line + role model" promotional mode. At the above working meeting, we also released the handbook (for trial) on the administration of experimental areas.

At the 2010 working meeting held in Jiaozuo, we proposed to "bring out the true effect of new education with concrete actions." In the same year, another working meeting of experimental areas was held in Huoqiu of Anhui Province. I gave a speech entitled "At the Starting Point for the Next Decade," exchanging ideas with the audience on the past, present, and future of the experiment. From 2012, nearly all the working meetings of experimental areas were held in underdeveloped rural and remote areas to better promote new education in these areas.

In July 2015, the New Exam Evaluation Institute of the New Education Academy released the Directive Evaluation Framework for the Development of New Education Experimental Areas and Schools, which was put into trial use in experimental areas. The framework consists of two levels of indicators, key points for evaluation, and the point value of each key point. Level-1 indicators reflect the organization and management (20 percent), key projects (50 percent), and achievements (30 percent), which are then broken down to measure basic guarantees, major research findings and the top ten actions, and the four changes to new education, respectively. As to the key points for evaluation, the framework intends to fully reflect the practice and experience, research findings, or thinking of each experimental area in carrying out each project.

First, the organization and management of the New Education Experiment covers the following aspects:

1. The organizational leadership: A leading group is in place headed by competent government officials or departmental heads to solve problems and difficulties encountered in the implementation of the experiment in a timely manner. It can meet regularly or on an as-needed basis.
2. Team building: A workshop or task force should be assembled for each experimental project. Practical promotional systems and sound operating mechanisms should also be in place.
3. Action plans: Action plans or implementation plans should be developed for the experiment. The work plan should be laid out at the beginning of a year, followed by mid-year review and year-end summary. The plan should be feasible.
4. Funding: There should be earmarked funds to support the implementation of action plans or meet the financial demands of the experiment in a timely manner. Necessary office area, supplies, or acceptable working conditions should be guaranteed.
5. Management of experimental subjects: The experimental subjects should be managed properly according to the *New Education Administrative Measures on Experimental Subjects*. Relevant information should be delivered or reported in a timely, accurate manner according to the requirements of the subject management authority. Attention should be paid to the collection, sorting, safekeeping, and usage of experimental materials. An archive room should be in place to keep the experimental materials.

6. Project management: Each experimental area or school should determine its own bottom line and measures for the management of each experimental project based on local reality and have a clear idea of how to develop and implement relevant courses with desired effect.

7. Model teachers: The role of model teachers should be valued. Each experimental area or school should have its own model teachers and create conditions or opportunities for their further development.

8. Model schools: Each experimental area should have its own key experimental school and each experimental school its own experimental class, with clearly defined priorities, favorable policy support, and effective measures.

9. Teacher training: Each experimental area or school should be able to launch effective teacher training or teaching research activities continuously, with attention paid to professional guidance, peer support, and self-reflection in school-based teaching research. The effect of such activities can be reflected in the data collected in the implementation process.

10. Open activities: Each experimental area or school should keep pace with the times and seek progress in light of local reality; actively participate in annual meetings, meetings of experimental areas, international forums on new education, and open-week activities launched in other experimental areas; and host its own open week on a regular or intermittent basis with distinct characteristics and desired effect.

Second, key projects of the New Education Experiment include:

1. Campus culture building:
   A. The ideological culture (including the educational philosophy, core values, mission, vision, school positioning, educational goals, motto, ethos, teaching style, learning style, school spirit, managerial philosophy, message from the principal, teachers' oath, and students' oath)
   B. The visual culture (including the school emblem, standard fonts, standard colors, school flag, uniforms, office supplies, and signage)
   C. The campus environment (the campus should be clean, tidy, fresh looking, bright and full of life; scientifically planned, reasonably allocated, and well-equipped; elegantly decorated; and a good place to study
   D. Code of conduct (the development of regulations and rules, the organization of thematic activities, school newspapers, and magazines, etc.)
   E. The new education environment (such as popularizing the terminology, main contents, and achievements of the New Education Experiment)
2. Teachers' professional development:
   A. Reading (the quantity and quality of reading)

    B. Writing (the quantity and quality of writing)

    C. Networking with other teachers and the professional development community

    D. Professional identification and mental status

3. Creating a campus full of the fragrance of books:

    A. Reading facilities (including libraries, reading rooms, and the quality and quantity of books available; whether the books chosen reflect students' interest and demand and are graded; the utilization of books recommended by the New Reading Institute)

    B. The new education child courses ("morning and noon reading and evening reflection"; the listening-reading-drawing-speech course; and the quality and quantity of reading)

    C. Reading activities (the methods and measures to promote reading, reading festivals, teacher–student reading, parent–child reading)

    D. The reading environment (a favorable reading environment on campus, integrating abundant reading resources, and organizing colorful reading activities)

4. Developing excellent curriculum:

    A. Guided by the new education idea on excellent curriculum and based on the national, local, and school-based curriculum, teachers conduct secondary development and integration of textbooks and seek innovation in the curriculum to improve class education.

    B. While delivering courses, teachers should guide students to gain experience; conduct collaborative learning; establish connection between knowledge, the outer world, and their inner world; translate knowledge learned into wisdom; and enrich their life.

    C. Based on life courses, citizenship courses, art courses, and intellectual courses, and supplemented with specialty courses, each teacher should make the most of local resources and conditions and consider the characteristics of students while making his or her own contribution to the excellent curriculum.

5. Creating the ideal classroom:

    A. Developing a sound value system for the class and constructing the class culture

    B. Creating the ideal classroom (including the class culture, class curriculum, class name, class emblem, class motto, and class anthem)

    C. Teachers, students, and parents reading, writing, and living together to create common language and codes. Each classroom has its own vision, culture, and courses; immerses teachers and students with all the great masterpieces and classics of the human society; and inspires them to strive for excellence and creation day by day.

6. Creating the ideal class:
   A. The engagement, affinity, integration, freedom, exercise, and extendibility of the ideal class
   B. The three standards of the ideal class: the effective application of the teaching framework; the action and exploration to discover the great beauty of knowledge; striking resonance between knowledge and the life of teachers and students
7. Teachers and students writing essays together:
   A. Teachers keep writing teaching journals, teaching cases and educational stories to reflect on the daily teaching and learning life, and promote teachers' professional development and students' independent development.
   B. Teachers and students writing and exchanging essays to have heart-to-heart conservation with each other and create a meaningful life together
   C. Incorporating writing into the daily life of teachers and students and making it a key means for them to reflect on school education and family education. By writing together and via verbal communication, teachers, students, and parents will be closer to each other and create a unique, wonderful life together.
8. Advancing one thing per month:
   A. Choosing the most important habits that will benefit students for the rest of their life.
   B. Starting from specific things and catering to the different characteristics of different graders by increasing the difficulty grade by grade.
   C. Incorporating citizenship education and life education through extensive thematic reading, thematic practice, thematic research, and thematic essay writing. Each experimental school should explore advancing one thing per month in light of its own conditions.
9. Building a digital community:
   A. Connecting every school, class, and individual and building the teaching management platform and the educational resources platform
   B. Strengthening the integration of online resources inside and outside the school, building an online learning community, and allowing teachers and students to study and exchange online
   C. Conducting experiments and thematic research with the help of networks
   D. Teachers opening blogs online, keeping records of their professional development or collecting materials on their subject, and actively exchanging and sharing with more teachers

10. Listening to the voice outside the window:
    A. Understanding the society and real social life through campus lectures, community activities, and public interest activities
    B. Making full use of community educational resources for learning, and guiding teachers and students to love life and care about the society
    C. Integrating resources of local communities and schools and inspiring teachers and students to embrace diverse values
    D. Actively participating in training and open-week activities on new education launched in experimental areas or nationwide; listening to the voice outside the window and improving oneself
11. Eloquence training:
    A. Encouraging teachers and students to speak and train their eloquence via various kinds of activities in school and in everyday life to help boost their confidence and improve their ability to express themselves and communicate with others
    B. Training teachers and students to be good listeners, which will increase their access to knowledge and information and increase their popularity as well
12. Family–school cooperation:
    A. Hosting regular activities for parents and students to bring them closer to the school and create an environment good for teenagers' harmonious and healthy development
    B. Actively participating in the experimental activities of the New Parents Institute
    C. Recommending books and magazines on family education to parents and organizing activities to create learning-oriented families and communities
    D. Actively launching projects for schools to work with parents in promoting students' growth, and creating a family–school relationship featuring interaction, communication, coordination, and agreement, to produce educational synergy and guiding students' improvement in moral qualities, behavior, and habits

Third, achievements of the New Education Experiment include:

1. Students' progress:
    A. Academic performance:
       i. Students in experimental schools have seen their scores significantly improved on the whole, and outperformed peers in nonexperimental schools.
       ii. Students' scores have been growing year by year.

      iii. Students in experimental schools have read more and better and significantly outperformed those in nonexperimental schools in reading.

      iv. Students in experimental schools have seen their writing skills significantly improved on the whole and have outperformed those in nonexperimental schools.

      v. Students in experimental schools have seen their eloquence significantly improved on the whole and have outperformed those in nonexperimental schools.

  B. All-around development:

      i. Students have become more upbeat, positive, happier, confident, and interested in learning.

      ii. Students identify themselves more with the school and are more content with their school life than peers in nonexperimental schools.

      iii. Students in experimental schools have seen their cultural and sports abilities significantly improved and have outperformed those in nonexperimental schools.

      iv. Students in experimental schools have seen their innovation thinking and ability significantly improved and have outperformed those in nonexperimental schools.

      v. Students in experimental schools have seen their awareness of exchange and cooperation significantly raised and have outperformed those in nonexperimental schools.

2. Teachers' growth:

  A. Team building:

      i. On the whole, teachers identify more with the teaching job, and become more motivated and enthusiastic at work.

      ii. Teachers are happier and feel their life fulfilled and valued compared with those in nonexperimental schools.

      iii. Teachers have seen their awareness of cooperation and coordination much enhanced and have outperformed those in nonexperimental schools.

      iv. The number of model teachers has been growing year by year.

      v. Model teachers have played a positive role in team building.

  B. Professional development:

      i. Teachers have read more and better and have significantly outperformed those in nonexperimental schools in reading.

      ii. Teachers have written more and better and have significantly outperformed those in nonexperimental schools in writing.

      iii. Teachers have researched more and better and have significantly outperformed those in nonexperimental schools in research.

3. Schools' achievements:
   A. Academic achievements: Some schools have published papers on experimental projects launched, or produced booklets or publications on their experimental findings; teaching research activities related to the experiment have been ongoing and growing in numbers year by year; teaching research activities related to the experiment have produced desired effects, with documents and videos collected and kept for archiving purposes.
   B. Campus culture building: While building the campus culture, schools have done a remarkable job in cultivating students' sentiment, guiding their behavior, raising their awareness of cultural legacy and teamwork, and fostering their sound character and individuality.
   C. Management achievements: Experimental schools have set up their own democratic, efficient management teams; school management has been greatly improved and is turning for the better.
4. Impact of the experiment:
   A. The awareness of engagement: Teachers and staff are generally familiar with the experiment and embrace the ideas of new education; the majority of them are glad to contribute to the experiment and are actively doing so. They are volunteering to study, promote, and practice the ideas of new education.
   B. Social impact: The progress of the experiment has been covered by journals and online media at the district level and above; experimental schools are better spoken of by parents than before and have seen their enrollment rate rising significantly. Community administrators show more support for experimental schools and are more content with their performance.
   C. Government support: Competent education authorities show much more acceptance for, satisfaction with, and support for new education.
   D. Peer impact: The experiment has attracted extensive attention and praise from education peers. Experimental schools are invited to share their practice, achievements, and experience in new education to non-experimental schools and play the demonstration role.

This framework is built on all the practices of new education experimental areas and schools. As its name suggests, it is intended to, with the help of all the indicators and key points of evaluation listed, guide experimental areas and schools to better carry out experimental activities through self-examination on one hand, and provide reference for administrators to help them better guide and aid the development of experimental areas and schools on the other.

In January 2017, the New Exam Evaluation Institute refined and improved the scheme and produced the Evaluation System for New Education

Experimental Schools (trial) to promote self-evaluation, self-examination, and self-improvement among experimental areas and schools.

II. Regional Practice and Exploration

For more than a decade, we have been relentlessly exploring creative ways to realize the new education ideal and have found the following effective approaches to promote new education on a regional scale.

i. Establishing a Common Vision to Mobilize People of the Same Mind

The New Education Experiment has been upholding the ideal of new education since the very beginning. In the academic pursuit, it aims to grow into a flag of education for all-around development in China on one hand and develop a new education school that is deeply rooted in Chinese society on the other. As to its core mission, it aims to help teachers and students create a happy, all-around educational life. Most of the experimental areas are attracted and inspired by the ideal of new education and have been deeply involved in the experiment.

ii. Introducing Innovative Mechanisms

Experimental areas across China are either formed through administrative promotion or by school alliances. In government-driven experimental areas, the experiment is generally included into the daily education administration work. Many education bureaus have added the implementation of the experiment to the evaluation program for local kindergartens and primary and middle schools, which has helped ensure the minimum engagement of schools in the experiment and motivated them to promote new education.

Haimen Experimental Area has summarized their experience in promoting new education as follows: cooperation and coordination between government departments responsible for ideological education, education administration, workshops and training, and supervision, and engagement of the municipal education bureau, education groups, and schools. For example, the primary education department of the education bureau is responsible for administrative coordination; the further studies center of primary and middle school teachers for advancing research on experimental projects and follow-up research on initiatives to create a campus full of the fragrance of books, the ideal classroom, and ideal class, developing excellent curriculum, and taking the experimental projects a step further; and the new education teachers' training center for providing training for teachers and projects to promote new education at the local level. These well-developed mechanisms help ensure the sound interaction between the municipal education bureau, education groups, and schools in carrying out experimental projects, and make sure these projects are advanced effectively in every experimental school in the region.

iii. Highlighting the Importance of Actions and Experimental Projects for the Experiment

The New Education Experiment is an education reform and experiment that creates impact mainly through the top ten actions and other experimental projects. Despite the varying intensity and priority in advancing the ten actions, experimental areas have reached the following consensus: creating a campus full of the fragrance of books is to enrich the spiritual life of teachers and students; helping students foster good habits is to help them improve themselves; creating the ideal class is to inject vitality into every class; creating the digital community is to provide a development platform for every teacher; building the campus culture is to foster the unique character of every experimental school; creating the ideal classroom is to turn classroom education into a source of happiness; developing excellent curriculum is to benefit every student with suitable courses; promoting family–school cooperation is to help every parent master the scientific way of family education. In addition, the "morning and noon reading and evening reflection" initiative promoted among children and the teachers' professional development mode have been widely promoted in experimental areas.

iv. Creating Platforms for Research and Exchange Activities

The colorful research and exchange activities are considered an important way to advance the New Education Experiment. They give teachers and students the chance to showcase their achievements and share experiences and what they have benefited from the experiment. Regional research and exchange activities are generally divided into four categories. First is routine activities. The New Education Experiment has been incorporated into the daily teaching research activities of experimental schools. Second is thematic activities. Education administrations and schools often hold thematic discussions or demonstrations on new education, including the discussion on the ideal classroom, the demonstration of excellent curriculum, and the semester opening and closing ceremonies. Third is thematic research activities. Thematic research projects of the New Education Experiment and of regional education science are applied to dig deeper into new education. Fourth is open week activities. Experimental areas such as Haimen in Jiangsu, Jiaozuo in Henan, Shijiazhuang in Hebei, Luoyang High & New Industry Development Zone in Henan, and Huanggu in Liaoning have hosted their respective open week on new education and opened it to the rest of the country, featuring the demonstration and discussion of the theme of annual meetings or key projects, to promote new education in other parts of the country.

v. Setting Role Models

Setting and promoting role models and playing out their leading role are an important strategy to promote new education in experimental areas. For more than ten years, experimental areas have produced a number of model schools, model principals, and model teachers. Their stories and spirit will inspire and guide many followers to move forward. At the annual meeting on new education, model teachers, ideal classrooms, and excellent curriculum of the year will be voted. The wise principal award has been issued since 2016. All these efforts have greatly advanced the New Education Experiment.

III. Case Studies

Since we laid down the regional promotion approach in 2005, the new education experimental areas have grown by about 10 in numbers year by year, greatly improving local education. Take Haimen in Jiangsu Province for example. In over a decade, the New Education Experiment has truly changed the life of teachers and students and continued to improve local education quality. In the summer vocation of 2012, Haimen selected 18 model readers to compete in a competition organized by the *Reading* program of CCTV-10, and four of them, namely Chen Shuqi, Cao Andong, Yu Jinwen, and Gu Renhao, made it to the finals for the country's top 30 contestants; Chen Shuqi and Gu Renhao made it to the country's top 10 contestants. In 2014, Ni Ziqiang, a student from Haimen Middle School, won the international competition of *Super Brain*. Dongzhou Primary School has claimed the championship of World Robot Contests for several years in a row. Hainan Primary School won second place in the league of the China University Football Association. Haimen Experimental Primary School won first place in the national school play contest and has topped the province in the quality of compulsory education and in the results of high school and college entrance exams for consecutive years. Over 20,000 educators from the rest of the country visit Haimen per year to learn from it and receive training on new education. Haimen's success in new education has made news on *China Education Daily*, *People's Education*, CCTV, *Xinhua Daily*, china.com.cn, people.com.cn, and gmw.cn. The New Education Experiment has become Haimen's signature project, showcasing its strength and beauty. Below is a case about how the New Education Experiment helped improve local education in a county in rural China.

The above section has drawn reference from the paper by Dr. Xu Xinhai published in the *Journal of the Chinese Society of Education*, Issue No. 5 of 2015.

New Education in Suixian County: Exploring an Alternative Path for Rural Education

Suixian County is said to be the birthplace of Emperor Yan and Shennong, and where the chime music was invented, enjoying a long-lasting history and rich cultural legacy. On the twenty-sixth day of the fourth lunar month every year, a day said to be the birthday of Emperor Yan, the provincial government of Hubei will host a memorial ceremony in Suixian to pay tribute to Emperor Yan. The municipal education bureau of Suizhou and the county education bureau of Suixian will stage the Chime Music Festival and the Cultural and Artistic Festival in Memory of Emperor Yan every other year for local primary and middle schools. Suixian didn't resume its county status until 2009. So far, the county infrastructure is still to be built and there is no urban school yet: all the 108 primary and middle schools across the county are located in rural areas, a rare case among county-level regions in China. Suixian never tries to turn away from the issue; instead it has been working hard to find a new development path suitable for rural education.

When fall turned into winter in 2009, a delegation from Suixian arrived in Jiangxian in Shanxi Province for the annual meeting on new education and has been following the latest development of the New Education Experiment since then. In the spring of 2011, Suixian decided to promote new education across the country. In September, it officially became a new education experimental area at the new education annual meeting held in Dongsheng. In the past six years, it has been endeavoring to promote new education in rural areas. This option has proved to be the most sensible because new education has injected strong vitality into rural education. The New Education Experiment has become the most powerful weapon of local education, and is quietly changing the rural education scene, the school development pattern, and the life of teachers and students.

i. Nurturing Rural Children Through the New Education Experiment
Left-behind children are a special group of rural children and a focus of rural education. An army of rural residents have moved to cities seeking after a better life, which has driven social progress and satisfied people's inner urge for a better life. But when the migrant workers leave, most of them leave their children behind at home, thus the name left-behind children. The absence of parents will surely affect children's growth.

In response, Suixian introduced new education actions to benefit the left-behind children. For example, meetings were organized for these children to share their experience in "morning and noon reading and evening reflection" and activities to nurture their heart and mind with poems and books recommended by the New Education Experiment, ease their mourning for being separated from their parents with the joy of sharing and exchange, and channel their negative moods caused by excessive yearning for the love of parents. Gradually the children become more independent and strong-minded.

On traditional festivals and holidays, the listening-reading-drawing-speech activities were organized for them. Children could take the opportunity to read out poems expressing gratitude to parents or articles remembering one's families or hometown, and then draw what they felt to ease their anxiety and depression. From time to time, children's cooking contests were held, and cooking became one of the most important parts of the one-thing-per-month initiative. Through such activities, the children learned to appreciate the value of food, the chance to show themselves and exchange with others, and the intense and interesting competitions, and learned to be proud of themselves. The sense of self-efficacy will motivate them to succeed, to seek truths and development by following their heart. The sense of self-efficacy and the experience of success are vital for education and the ultimate reason for education. In this way, education happens before anyone realizes it. Huo Lili, a left-behind child in Xinjie Township Central School, joined the "One of My Extracurricular Books" campaign hosted by CCTV and made it to the final 18. All of these are the fruits of Suixian's efforts in creating a campus full of the fragrance of books, selecting teenage readers, and promoting thematic reading.

Family–school cooperation realized through the new parents committee is an important way to nurture rural children. By establishing the parents' lecture system, advocating parent–child reading, and holding parents' meetings on family education, Suixian has extended education from campus to home, turned purposeless family education into purposeful, organized family education with pertinent contents, and filled in the blanks of family education through family–school collaborative actions to benefit rural children.

ii. Carrying Forward Rural Culture Through the New Education Experiment

Suixian County consists of 18 rural towns, and rural culture is one of the most important parts of local education. To develop rural education is not to erase the impact of rural culture, but to preserve and carry forward elements in rural culture that agree with values of contemporary society. While promoting new education, Suixian pays particular attention to digging out rural culture, incorporating it into education, and turning it into an educational asset, so as to enrich educational contents with rural culture, inherit and carry forward rural culture through education, and allow the two to integrate with and reinforce each other. For this purpose, Suixian has developed a course on the legacy of Emperor Yan, built a cultural site and designated a cultural inheritance base school dedicated to Emperor Yan, and launched a patriotism education base in Emperor Yan's hometown scenic area in partnership with the local steering committee. In this way, it has blended the local culture with rural characteristics and the farming tradition. The Yiyang tune is the most famous intangible cultural heritage of Wanhe Town in Suixian, known for its special singing tune. Yiyang Primary School is a designated school for the inheritance of the Yiyang tune, and teacher Cai Xiufen the designated inheritor. She has taught generations of students to perform the Yiyang tune and write lyrics, to enhance their eloquence and artistic attainments.

In addition, Suixian has designated schools as inheritance and promotion bases for the flower-drum opera and the chime music, and included the bench dragon and playing diabolo, two traditional local entertainments, into the sports and artistic activities on campus. Folk art has thus become an integral part of rural new education. By so doing, education is advanced through rural culture and rural traditional folk culture and art that are almost forgotten are given new life through education. Courses are developed based on and to promote rural culture. Suixian has developed courses on the cultural legacy of Emperor Yan, on seeds, on stone mosaic, on growth ceremonies, on traditional games for rural children, and on farming experience, successively. Each of these courses is the embodiment of rural culture. Emperor Yan was the father of the farming culture, and seeds and farming skills are the most essential for rural and agricultural development. Traditional games for rural children are also part of rural culture and the daily life of local students. The course on growth ceremonies is another mirror of folk culture in Suixian.

By combining the rustic, local culture with education through new education actions, Suixian has found an effective way to highlight the features of rural education and improve its quality.

iii. Awakening Rural Teachers Through the New Education Experiment

Reading, writing, and professional networking are three treasures for the professional development of teachers. Suixian has organized reading salons, writing platforms, lectures on teachers' professional development, and a professional development community as platforms for teachers to exchange and network with each other. Reading is the touchstone for teachers' professional development. The more a teacher reads on his subject, the clearer a picture he will have of the subject.

Reading is a must-take route toward the ideal. Suixian has organized thematic reading salons and would recommend a book for participants to read from time to time. For example, by reading the book *New Education*, teachers can learn the three standards for the ideal class, apply the knowledge to classroom teaching, and exchange their ideas and experience in this regard. This is a case of combining theory reading with practice. To create the ideal class, teachers would demonstrate the ideal class patterns, namely, the happy class, the smart class, and the efficient class, respectively for primary schools, junior high schools, and high schools and exchange their experience. Then they would vote the ideal class pattern for three-dimensional collaboration and health education. Based on that, Suixian has formulated Guiding Opinions on the Class Education Reform, designated the year of efficient class education, and organized the ideal class exhibition in order to strike deep resonance between knowledge and life.

Reading and writing for sharing with others are an exchange of thoughts. Suixian has organized a team named the Flames and Seeds of Education to advocate reading, writing, and exchange on a daily basis. Lectures on the cultural legacy of Emperor Yan were given across the county, and online platforms created to promote teachers' reading, writing, and networking. QQ groups, WeChat groups, Weibo posts, and blogs were employed to awaken and arouse the passion among a group of seed teachers, to stimulate them to go further on the path of professional development, to read more and deeper on their subject, and create a happier, all-around educational life. Meanwhile, role models are selected and promoted to guide the professional development of rural teachers. In Suixian, teacher Wang Conglun, aged 57, has guided students of the Sunshine Class to read at least six million Chinese characters per semester and developed a course on stone mosaic, which has become a signature course of rural education. Teacher Zhi Yongmei of the Four-Leaf Clover Class has cast the seeds of charity among the hearts of her students. There are more people like them, such as principal Wang Jun, teacher Liu Jinchao of the Dream Chaser Class, and teacher Zhang Cheng of the Firefly Class—they are all committed to new education and to the pursuit of a happy, all-around educational life. No matter how far they have gone, they never forget why they started. Many teachers in Suixian have published books and won national and provincial awards, and their stories have appeared in *China Teacher Paper*, *Hubei Education*, and *Educator*.

iv. Boosting Rural School Development Through the New Education Experiment

The New Education Experiment advocates campus culture as the soul of a school. A meaningful campus culture is a sign of the school's soft power and one of the three drives of Suixian's promotion of new education, the other two being moral education and class education. By introducing innovative projects in moral education, selecting outstanding patterns of class education, and building campus culture, Suixian has managed to bring local education and school development to a new high.

First, the building of campus culture is combined with efforts to create a campus full of the fragrance of books and create the ideal classroom so as to nurture the spiritual cultivation of teachers and students. The purpose is to promote reading on campus and turn the classroom and the campus into a paradise for children. Secondly, the classroom education reform is combined with efforts to create the ideal class and develop excellent curriculum. As a result, the class gravity is shifted from teaching to learning, and teachers change from curriculum "practitioners" to "developers" to inject vitality into school life and students' individuality. Thirdly, moral education is combined with efforts to advance one thing per month and promote family–school cooperation in order to consolidate the foundation for the happy, all-around education life of teachers and students, and promote students' healthy, harmonious development. Meanwhile social forces are also mobilized to engage in thematic activities to augment and enhance the educational function and contribute to social harmony through campus harmony.

Lishan No. 3 Middle School advocates the culture of "harmony," including teaching-learning harmony embodied in the class education pattern of three-dimensional collaboration, and harmony of physical and mental development through reading projects.

Shangshi No. 2 Middle School promotes the "sunshine" culture, consisting of sunshine classes, sunshine classrooms, and farming courses, casting the light of life on every corner of the campus. Jingming Primary School is committed to "harmony and elegance" of rural artistic education. Shangshi Township Primary School is after authenticity, including the authenticity of teachers and students, that of class education, and that of curriculum, in order to realize the original purpose of education.

Yindian Dongpo Middle School combines calligraphy with moral education, teaching students virtues such as compliance, broad-mindedness, and ingenuity by explaining the composition and structure of Chinese characters and the rules of calligraphy writing.

Caodian Township Primary School encourages students to enjoy trying, to stimulate their curiosity about the unknown.

As the New Education Experiment unfolds, schools attach more importance to reading and the characteristics of local rural culture. In 2013, Suixian passed the provincial evaluation of balanced development of compulsory education, and in 2014 it scored high in the national review. Experts agreed in the evaluation that "Suixian boasts educational soft power and contents superior to its schooling conditions and facilities." In 2015, *China Teacher Paper* published the article "The New Educational Scene of 108 Rural School" to acknowledge Suixian's progress in new education. In 2016, *Hubei Education* gave a detailed account of Suixian's practice in boosting rural development. The tenth issue of *Educator* in 2015 tracked Suixian's progress in advancing the New Education Experiment on the whole. In 2015, in the municipal comprehensive educational evaluation launched by Suizhou City, 23 of the top 30 junior middle schools were from Suixian, as were seven from the top 10. The case of Suixian has proved what changes new education can bring to rural education.

The above case on New Education in Suixian County: Exploring an Alternative Path for Rural Education from pages 165–170 is contributed by Zhang Huatao and Li Zhouwei from the New Education Workshop of Suixian New Education Experimental Area.

Social Evaluation

The New Education Experiment is a completely voluntary, bottom-up non-governmental initiative, a behavior research project of Chinese characteristics on education for all-around development during the key stage of child development. It has an ideal, passion, and takes actions to create the poetic life. Its four changes, five guiding principles, six theories, and seven actions are of Chinese characteristics.

—Yan Wenfan, professor and director of the Department of Leadership in Education, University of Massachusetts, Boston

The possibility to solve the problems we face in the twenty-first century is nurtured in the education reform of the New Education Experiment.

—Manabu Sato, former professor of Tokyo University, Japan

He is a "leading change maker" for what he does in China is a great, future-oriented, innovative, transformable, and sustainable undertaking that "leads to changes into the education mechanism and creates a beautiful future."

—Dr. Huang Quanyu, former director of the Asian/Asian American Studies Program, Miami University of Ohio

Tangerine is the color of wisdom, a great color for new education.

—Tan Swie Hian, Singaporean writer and artist, Member-Correspondent of the Academie des Beaux-Arts of France

I firmly believe that the encounter of the vibrant new education approach and the world's longest-standing traditions in China will give birth to something new.

—Benjamin Cherry, Australian educator, Asian coordinator of Waldorf Education

New education hasn't grown into a big oak tree yet, but will grow into a dense oak forest in the foreseeable future as teachers continue to practice and refine the ideas of new education.

—Dr. William Y. Lan, tenured professor of the College of Education, Texas Tech University

The practice (the New Education Experiment) is not a sweeping movement, but a down-to-earth reform driving social progress. I really appreciate professor Zhu Yongxin's spirit to advance the education reform in a down-to-earth, step-by-step way.

—Dr. Wang Zhixin, research fellow of the Institute for Advanced Studies in Education, Waseda University, director-general of Japan Association for International Exchange of Chui Fook Culture, and Ph.D. of pedagogy, Tokyo University

The mission of new education is to change China's education by promoting reading and broadening students' mind and vision. The New Education Experiment is against knowledge cramming, but encourages students to read, and teachers and students to write and exchange their essays so that they could really enjoy and realize the original purpose of education. Bearing this mission in mind, the new education movement, via communication platforms such as the Internet and the Education Online website, has attracted hundreds of primary and middle schools across the country in just a few years. Thanks to the concerted efforts of the New Education Experiment team and hundreds of experimental schools, the movement is growing into one of the leaders of China's education reform.

—Professor Suwa Tetsuo of Gakushuin University, Japan, author of *The Boiling Education Reform in China* (Japanese)

Chronicles of the New Education Experiment

I. Initiation (from September 1999 to September 2002)

In 1999, Zhu Yongxin was touched by a sentence from the book *The World According to Peter Drucker*, which went like this: "theory alone is not enough for you to be remembered by generations to come unless you do change and affect people's life." From then on, he started to teach in Hutangqiao Primary School in Jiangsu Province to practice his teachings.

In 2000, Zhu Yongxin published the book *My Educational Ideal*, proposing the initial thoughts and principles of the New Education Experiment.

In early 2002, the education experiment was officially named the New Education Experiment after rounds of discussion.

In June that year, *My Educational Ideal* was amended and republished under the title *The Dream of New Education*.

On June 18, Education Online was launched as the official website of the experiment, with Li Zhenxi as the chief webmaster.

In September, Yufeng Experimental School in Kunshan started to practice new education and became the first new education experimental school on October 28 when the inauguration ceremony was hosted.

II. Exploration (from September 2002 to July 2013)

In July 2003, the first seminar of the New Education Experiment was convened in Yufeng Experimental School in Kunshan.

In November that year, the New Education Experiment Research Center was founded in Yufeng Experimental School. Its daily affairs were run by the secretariat, with Secretary General Chu Changlou responsible for general coordination, Deputy Secretary General Zhang Rongwei for theoretical research, Yuan Weixing for marketing, and Zhou Xianhua for school liaison.

In April 2004, the second seminar of the New Education Experiment and the initiation meeting for the research project on the practice and promotion of new education theories, a key national research project in the education science during the Tenth Five-Year Plan period, was held in Zhangjiagang Advanced Middle School and Hutangqiao Central Primary School in Changzhou.

In September 2004, driven by local governments, Jiangyan City of Jiangsu Province and Qiaoxi District of Shijiazhuang in Hebei Province became the first new education experimental areas in China.

From July 31 to August 1, 2004, the third seminar of the New Education Experiment was staged in Baoying County, Yangzhou City of Jiangsu Province.

In October 2004, the New Education Experiment assembled the "6 + 1" project team for its six top actions and improved its organizational structure. The leading research team was run by the secretariat, with Chu Changlou as secretary general. The project team was composed of heads of the six top actions and the New Parents School. The theoretical research division of the leading research team was spun off to form the New Education Research Center, responsible for theoretical research, and headed by Zhang Rongwei.

In July 2005, the fourth seminar of the New Education Experiment took place in Yandao Street Foreign Language School in Chengdu, Sichuan Province, themed on new citizenship and life education. *The Handbook for the New Education Experiment* was published.

In December 2005, the fifth seminar of the New Education Experiment took place in Jilin No. 1 Experimental Primary School, themed on teachers' professional development.

In February, April, and May of 2006, Wei Zhiyuan, Gan Guoxiang, and Ma Ling joined the New Education Research Center, respectively.

In April 2006, Lu Zhiwen joined the management team and prepared to set up a new management agency.

In July 2006, the sixth seminar of the New Education Experiment took place in Tsinghua University, proposing that the core mission of new education was to "create a happy, all-around educational life." *The Handbook for the New Education Experiment* was amended and published.

In July 2007, the seventh seminar of the New Education Experiment took place in Yuncheng of Shanxi Province, calling for teachers and students to "read, write, and live together."

In September 2007, the working meeting of new education experimental areas was convened in Xiaoshan, Hangzhou of Zhejiang Province, announcing the founding of the New Education Academy, headed by Lu Zhiwen.

In November 2007, the New Education Research Association—Special Committee for the New Education Experiment of Jiangsu Education Association was officially inaugurated in Haimen, headed by Xu Xinhai.

In July 2008, the eighth seminar of the New Education Experiment took place in Cangnan County, Wenzhou of Zhejiang Province, themed on "deep resonance between knowledge and life."

In July 2009, the ninth seminar was held in Haimen of Jiangsu Province, themed on "writing the life legends of teachers." Five reference books including the *Handbook for Advancing One Thing per Month under the New Education Experiment* were published.

In September 2009, the Online Teachers College was opened, with Zhu Yongxin as president and Gan Guoxiang as executive president.

In November 2009, the working meeting of experimental areas was held in Jiangxian, Shanxi Province.

In February 2010, Jiangsu Changming Education Foundation (or the New Education Foundation) was registered, with Lu Zhiwen as director-general.

In July 2010, the tenth seminar of the New Education Experiment was held in Qiaoxi District of Shijiazhuang, themed on "culture—the soul of a school."

In September 2010, the New Reading Institute was opened in Beijing, with Wang Lin as president and Zhu Yinnian as executive president.

In September 2010, the New Education Academy inked the cooperation agreement with Dongsheng District Education Bureau of Ordos, Inner Mongolia, to jointly develop the Hantai New Education Experimental School.

In November 2010, the working meeting of experimental areas was held in Jiaozuo, Henan Province.

In July 2011, the first international summit on new education was held in Changzhou, Jiangsu Province, themed on "in the field of education."

In September 2011, the eleventh seminar of the New Education Experiment took place in Dongsheng District of Ordos, Inner Mongolia, themed on "living up to the true spirit of Chinese culture."

In November 2011, the New Education Parent–Child Reading Research Center was founded in Beijing, later renamed the New Parents Institute, with Tong Xixi as president and Lan Mei and Zhang Shuoguo as vice presidents. The Firefly Parent–Child Reading Project was launched.

In January 2012, the New Evaluation and Examination Institute, headed by Zhang Yong, and the New Vocational Education Research Center, headed by Shan Qiang, were opened under the New Education Academy.

In July 2012, the twelfth seminar of the New Education Experiment took place in Linzi, Shandong Province, themed on "creating the ideal classroom."

In October 2012, the second international summit on new education took place in Ningbo, Zhejiang Province, themed on "education and cultural reconstruction," announcing to increase the six top actions into ten.

In December 2012, the working meeting of experimental areas took place in Huoqiu, Anhui Province.

In January 2013, the New Education Council was reelected, with Xu Xinhai appointed as president and Chen Dongqiang vice president of the New Education Academy, and Lu Zhiwen as director-general of the New Education Foundation.

In July 2013, the thirteenth seminar of the New Education Experiment took place in Xiaoshan of Zhejiang Province, themed on "developing excellent curriculum," proposing the new education curriculum framework into which new citizenship education, new artistic education, new intellectual education, and individuality education were introduced on top of the new life education.

III. Deepening (since July 2013)

In April 2013, Haimen New Education Training Center was opened.

In November 2013, the third international summit on new education was convened in Chengdu, themed on "the power of reading."

In April 2014, the working meeting of new education experimental areas was held in Qingyang, Gansu Province.

In July 2014, the fourteenth seminar of the New Education Experiment took place in Suzhou, themed on "artistic education for the all-around development of people." A dozen books on new education including the *Annual Master Report on New Education* and *The Amazing Teachers* were published.

In November 2014, the fourth international summit on new education was staged in Rizhao, Shandong Province, themed on "constructing the ideal class."

In January 2015, Beijing Normal University hosted the seminar on creating the ideal classroom of the New Education Experiment sponsored by the Chinese Society of Education.

In the same month, Suzhou University founded the New Education Academy, which was headed by Xu Qingyu, dean of the College of Education.

In April 2015, the Academic Affairs Committee of the New Education Experiment was set up.

In May 2015, the working meeting of experimental areas was held in Kuitun, Xinjiang, during which the Chinese Society for Tao Xingzhi Studies founded the new education branch.

In June 2015, the New Family Education Academy and Qtone Education Group co-founded the New Family Education Academy, with Tong Xixi as director general, Sun Yunxiao as president, and Lan Mei as vice president.

In July 2015, the fifteenth seminar of the New Education Experiment took place in Jintang, Sichuan Province, themed on "increase the length, width, and height of life." Meanwhile *To Teachers* and *Guarding New Education* were published, adding to the new education book series.

In the same month, Yan Wenfan was appointed director of the New Education Research Center and Li Yihua deputy director. Mei Zihan, a famous children's literature writer, a promoter of child reading, and professor of Shanghai Normal University, was appointed president of the New Reading Institute, with Li Yiman and Li Xixi as vice presidents, successively.

In September 2015, the leadership of the Online Teachers College was reelected, with Zhu Yongxin as president and Li Zhenxi executive vice president.

In November 2015, the fifth international summit on new education took place in Zhengzhou, Henan Province, themed on "developing excellent curriculum."

In February 2016, the New Life Research Institute was founded under the New Education Academy, with Feng Jianjun as director and Yuan Weixing as executive director.

In April 2016, the working meeting of experimental areas took place in Suixian, Hubei Province.

In January 2016, the New Education Academy stopped publishing *New Education—Reading, Writing and Life*, and launched *Education—Reading, Writing and Life*.

In July 2016, the sixteenth seminar of the New Education Experiment took place in Zhucheng, Shandong Province, themed on "habit is the second nature." And the *Handbook on Advancing One Thing per Month—Fostering Good Habits That Will Benefit the Rest of Your Life*, *Thirty-Six Movie Lectures towards Good Habits—The Project Book for Advancing One Thing per Month*, *Life-Illuminating Education*, and *Between the Family and the School—Teaching Students of Junior Class* were published, adding to the new education book series.

In the same month, the New Education Development Center was opened, with Xu Xinhai as director, and Zhang Bingchen and Zhang Chuanruo as deputy directors.

In September 2016, the textbook series *Morning Reading of New Education* and *New Life Education* were published.

In November 2016, the sixth international summit on new education took place in Wenzhou of Zhejiang Province, themed on "future schools."

In April 2017, the working meeting of experimental areas was organized in Beichuan, Sichuan Province.

In May 2017, the New Education Academy co-developed the new-generation app for new education with Chaoxing Group.

In July 2017, the seventeenth seminar of the New Education Experiment took place in Qixia, Nanjing of Jiangsu Province, themed on "family–school cooperation."

In November 2017, the international summit on new education was held in Haimen New Education Experimental Area in Jiangsu, themed on "casting the seeds of science," attracting the participation of experts from the United States, Australia, New Zealand, and across the Taiwan Strait.

So far, the New Education Experiment has covered all mainland provinces, municipalities directly under the central government, and autonomous regions in China. It was voted among the top 15 competing for the World Innovation Summit for Education (WISE) award of the Qatar Foundation in 2014 and won the Fourth National Typical Case of Innovation in Education Award conferred by *China Education Daily* in 2015. The new education team has been publishing journals such as *Education—Reading, Writing and Life* and *Research and Review on Education*, and the new education book series of more than 100 titles, and won numerous awards. In particular, the 16-volume *Works by Zhu Yongxin on Education* has been translated into English, Korean, Japanese, French, and Arabic and exported to overseas markets.

Postscript

This book was written as part of the *Book Series on the Reform and Innovation in Education in Contemporary China* upon the request by the Renmin University of China Press.

Four years ago, editor Wang Xueying asked me to serve as the chief editor for a book series on the reality of education reform in contemporary China, but back then I was too busy with my job at the Central Committee of China Association for Promoting Democracy, the promotion of the New Education Experiment, and the compilation of the *Overview of Education Reform in China*.

After the *Overview of Education Reform in China* was released at the beginning of this year, Ms. Wang came to me again, asking me to produce a popular version of the *Overview*, which I declined once again due to my tight schedule.

But before long, I read news about China's math textbooks and teaching methods for primary school students being introduced into the UK. Then Xueying and the leaders of the press visited me once again at the Central Committee of China Association for Promoting Democracy, hoping that we could tell the world what's happening in China's education scene as it was.

They reminded me of the 2015 BBC documentary "Are Our Kids Tough Enough? Chinese School," which features the cultural clash between Chinese and British teachers and students, and how they overcome the difference and triumph in math, science, and Chinese exams. I came to appreciate the meaning of this job. Indeed, education has played a vital role in China's economic miracle, but China's education remains a mystery to the outside world. We need to share with other people in the world stories about China's education and enrich and improve our education in the exchange process.

So I said yes this time, agreeing to organize experts to compile the *Book Series on the Reform and Innovation in Education in Contemporary China*, including this one, *The New Education Experiment: Exploring an Alternative Path of Education for China*.

To my surprise, the press hoped to release this book at Beijing International Book Fair in August 2017 to kick-start the book series.

Time was ticking, and it was too late to find the right authors and edit their contribution to keep the style consistent and avoid repeated content, so I decided to write this book by myself, which I finished in more than two months. It should be pointed out that though this book is published in my name, it is a collective work of the new education community; so is the New Education Experiment. New education is nothing you say or write, but what you do.

I am indebted to all the new education experimental areas, schools, and model teachers for supplying a host of materials and stories, which inspired this book. I want to thank Xu Xinhai, Lu Zhiwen, Chen Dongqiang, and Tong Xixi of the New Education Council; the Firefly and Seed Team of new education teachers; and Yu Guozhi, Xue Xiaozhe, Du Tao, and Teng Jingnan for providing precious photos for this book. My thanks also go to editor Wang Xueying of the Renmin University of China Press for her hard work to make this book possible.

Zhu Yongxin
July 29, 2017
Dripping-Stone Studio, Beijing

Index

CPSIA information can be obtained
at www.ICGtesting.com
Printed in the USA
LVHW012041050220
645949LV00012B/1070